ISBN 978-1-330-81071-2
PIBN 10108423

This book is a reproduction of an important historical work. Forgotten Books uses state-of-the-art technology to digitally reconstruct the work, preserving the original format whilst repairing imperfections present in the aged copy. In rare cases, an imperfection in the original, such as a blemish or missing page, may be replicated in our edition. We do, however, repair the vast majority of imperfections successfully; any imperfections that remain are intentionally left to preserve the state of such historical works.

1 MONTH OF
FREE
READING

at

www.ForgottenBooks.com

By purchasing this book you are eligible for one month membership to ForgottenBooks.com, giving you unlimited access to our entire collection of over 700,000 titles via our web site and mobile apps.

To claim your free month visit:
www.forgottenbooks.com/free108423

English
Français
Deutsche
Italiano
Español
Português

www.forgottenbooks.com

Mythology Photography **Fiction**
Fishing Christianity **Art** Cooking
Essays Buddhism Freemasonry
Medicine **Biology** Music **Ancient
Egypt** Evolution Carpentry Physics
Dance Geology **Mathematics** Fitness
Shakespeare **Folklore** Yoga Marketing
Confidence Immortality Biographies
Poetry **Psychology** Witchcraft
Electronics Chemistry History **Law**
Accounting **Philosophy** Anthropology
Alchemy Drama Quantum Mechanics
Atheism Sexual Health **Ancient History**
Entrepreneurship Languages Sport
Paleontology Needlework Islam
Metaphysics Investment Archaeology
Parenting Statistics Criminology
Motivational

THE

ANGLO-SAXON VERSION

OF THE

LIFE OF ST. GUTHLAC,

Hermit of Crowland.   c. 730

ORIGINALLY WRITTEN IN LATIN, BY

FELIX (COMMONLY CALLED) OF CROWLAND.

Now first printed from a MS. in the Cottonian Library.

WITH A TRANSLATION AND NOTES,

BY

CHARLES WYCLIFFE GOODWIN, M.A.

FELLOW OF CATHARINE HALL, CAMBRIDGE.

LONDON:

JOHN RUSSELL SMITH,

4, OLD COMPTON STREET, SOHO SQUARE.

MDCCCXLVIII.

1848

35027

C. AND J. ADLARD, PRINTERS, BARTHOLOMEW-CLOSE.

5¹ ep

PREFACE.

THE Life of St. Guthlac, Hermit of Crowland, was originally written in Latin by one Felix, of whom nothing is with certainty known, further than what appears upon the face of his work.* From its being dedicated to Alfwold, king of the East-Angles, it may be conjectured that the author was an inmate of some monastery within the realm of East-Anglia; and he cannot have written later than A. D. 749,—the year of Alfwold's death. Though not personally acquainted with Guthlac, Felix drew his materials from persons who had known and conversed with the saint, and notwithstanding the

* The Latin Life is printed both in the Bollandine and Benedictine Acta Sanctorum, under the 11th of April. Felix is usually called a monk of Crowland. In one MS. he is termed in the prologue, Catholicæ Congregationis Sancti Bedan vernaculus, from which the Benedictine editor infers that he was a monk of Jarrow. But this reading is unsupported by other MSS., and no dependence can be placed upon it.

marvellous colouring given to the incidents related, the memoir may be regarded as, upon the whole, authentic, and as a curious picture of the belief and habits of the age.

Upon the work of Felix is founded the poetical Legend of St. Guthlac, contained in that singular collection of Anglo-Saxon poetry the Codex Exoniensis. Less important, but not without its value to the student of our ancient literature, is the prose version in the same language, now for the first time given to the public. When and by whom this translation was made is unknown; the style is not that of Ælfric, to whom it has been groundlessly ascribed. The florid rhetoric of Felix is much pruned and cropped, but without the omission of any material incidents; the writer often paraphrases rather than translates, and in truth sometimes quite mistakes sense of the original.

Only one MS. of this version is known to exist, preserved in the Cottonian collection, in the volume marked Vespasian Ð. xxi. But amongst the contents of the MS. known as the Codex Vercellensis is an extract comprising two chapters of the Life of Guthlac. For a transcript of this most interestin

PROLOGUE.

TO the truly-believing in our Lord, for ever and ever, to my dearest lord above all other men, earthly kings:—Alfwold, king of the East-Angles, rightly and worthily holding the kingdom:—I, Felix, have set forth the true belief, and the blessing of eternal salvation for all God's faithful people, and send greeting. Thy words and commands I have obeyed; the book which thou bespakest I have composed, concerning the life of Guthlac, of venerable memory, with clear words and testimonies. I therefore beg and beseech the learned and the faithful, if he here find any ridiculous phrase, that he blame us not before. But let each of these censorious and derisive persons reflect and consider that God's kingdom standeth not in [eloquence] but in stead-fastness of the holy faith; and reflect and consider that the salvation of earth was not devised with light thoughts, but was preached and declared by fishermen. And if any man censure our attempt

man urc angin and weorc tǽle (swa ic menige
wat on Angel-cynne mid þam fægerum stafum gegylde, fægere[1] and glǽwlice gesette, þæt hig þas
boc sylfe[2] settan mihton), ne wite he þonne us
swa [we][3] neode and hǽse gehyrsumodon[4] and
word gefyldon. Forþan lá þu leornere gif þu mid
þan þeawe tælendra me hleahtrige, warna þe sylfne
þær þu þe hleahtres wene, þæt þu þær semninga ne
wurðe mid dymnysse þystro ablend. Þæt bið
blindra þeaw þonne hi[5] on leohte beoð, þæt hig
sylfe nyton buton hi on þeostrum dwelion. On
halgum gewrihtum bið oft unwisdom [blindnes][6]
geciged, forþon se fruma ealles yfeles ærest þonan
cymð. For þisum þingum þonne þu leornere ic þe
manige þæt þu þa fremdan ne tǽle, þelǽs þu fram
oþrum eft swá fremde getæled sig. Ac þylǽs ic
lenge þone þanc hefige þara leornendra mid gesegenum þara fremdra tælnysse, swa swa ic[7] strange
sǽ and mycele oferliðe, and nu becume to þære
smyltestan hyðe, Guðlaces lifes. Forþon þu abǽde
æt me þæt ic þe write and sǽde be þære drohtnunge
Guðlaces and his lifes bysene, ic þe forþon hyrsumode and ic forþon write swa me þa dihteras sǽdon
þe his lif geornost cuðon; ærost hwylc wǽre se
fruma oþþe on hwylcum ende hé hit eft gelǽdde.
For þisum þingum ic þas boc[8] sette; þæt þa þe his
lif þæs cadigan weres cuðon, þæt him þonne þig

---

[1] MS. fæger. [2] MS. sylf. [3] [we] not in MS. [4] MS. gehyrsum.
[5] MS. he. [6] [blindnes] not in MS. [7] MS. sco. [8] MS. bec.

and work (as I know many in England who might
have written this book themselves, gilded with fair
letters, fairly and cleverly composed), let him not
blame us who have but obeyed compulsion and command, and fulfilled an order. Therefore, O! learner,
if thou deridest me after the manner of censurers,
take heed to thyself, lest whilst thou thinkest of
laughter, thou become suddenly blinded by the obscurity of darkness. It is the manner of blind
men when they are in the light, that they know
not but that they wander in the dark. In the holy
Scriptures folly is often called [blindness], because
from thence comes the beginning of all evil. For
this cause I admonish thee, O! learner, that thou
censure not strangers, lest thou be afterwards as a
stranger censured by others. But lest I longer
weary the mind of learners by talking of the censure
of strangers, I sail as it were over a strong and
mighty sea, and now come to that most quiet haven,
the life of Guthlac. As thou didst require of me
that I should write and relate concerning the conversation of Guthlac and the example of his life, I
have accordingly obeyed thee, and I write as those
informants told me who knew his life most accu-
rately; in the first place what was its beginning,
and then to what end he brought it. For this
cause I have composed this book, that as for those
who knew the life of the blessed man they may be

geneahhor his lifes to gemyndum come; and þam
oðrum þe hit ær ne cuþon swá swá ic him rúmne
weg and geradne tæhte.   Þas þingc þe ic her on-
write, ic geleornode fram gesegenum þæs arwyrðan
abbodes Wilfrides.   Swilc eac manige oðre me þæt
sædon, þe mid þam eadigan were wæron and his lif
hira eagum ofersawon. · Ne tweoge ic aht þa mine
dihteras þæt hi mihton gemunan and eall asecgan
þa wundru þises eadigan weres; wæron hi swiðe
wide cuðe and mære geond Angel-cynnes land.   Ic
forþon þinum bebodum hyrsumede and þin word
and willan hæbbe gefylled and þæt gewrit þisse
andweardan hyrde swá ic mihte mid wisdome minra[1]
foregengena and þæra[2] yldrena gesette; þone fruman
on þam fruman ic gesette, and þone ende in þam
ende.

[1] MS. minre.   [2] MS. þære.

the more abundantly reminded of his life; and that to others who knew it not before, I might as it were point out a wide and straight way. The things which I here write, I learned from the relation of the venerable abbot Wilfrid. Also many others have related it to me who were with the blessed man, and saw his life with their own eyes. Nor doubt I aught that my informants were able to remember and relate all the wonders of this blessed man; they were very widely known and famous through England. I accordingly have obeyed thy commands, and have fulfilled thy word and will, and I have composed the text of this present book, as I best might, with the wisdom of my predecessors and their elders; the beginning I have put in the beginning, and the end at the end.

I.

ON þam dagum Æþelredes þæs mæran kyninges
Myrcna, was sum æþel[1] man on þære heh-þeode
Myrcna-rice; se wæs haten Penwald. He wæs þæs
yldestan and þæs æþelstan cynnes þe Iclingas wæron
genemnede. He wæs for worulde welig and myccle
gestreon hæfde, and þaþa he welegost wæs and
mæst gestreon hæfde, ða gyrnde he him his ge-
mæccan to nymanne. He him þa ana geceas on
þæra[2] mædena heape þe þær fægorost wæs and
æþelestan kynnes; seo wæs gehaten Tette : and hi
þa samod wæron oð þone fyrst þæt God foresceawode
þæt þæt wif mid bearne geeacnod wæs. Ða se tíma
com þæt heo þæt bearn cennan scolde, þa sæmninga
com tacn of heofenum, and þæt bearn[3] swytelice
mid inseglum beclysde : efne, men· gesawon ane
hand on þam fægerestan readan hiwe of heofonum
cumende; and seo hæfde ane gyldene róde, and
wæs æteowod manegum mannum, and helde toweard
toforan þæs huses duru þær þæt cild inne acenned
wæs. Ða men þa ealle þe þæt gesawon þiderweard
efeston þæt hig þæt tacen swutelicor geseon woldon
and ongitan. Seo hánd þa gewende mid þære róde
up to heofonum. Ða men þa ealle þe þæt tacen
gesawon, hi hi þa ealle on eorðan astrehton, and
God bǽdon þæt he heom geswutelian scolde hwæt
þæt tacn and þæt forebeacn beon scolde þe him þær

---

[1] MS. æþela.   [2] MS. þære.   [3] MS. tacn.

I.

IN the days of Æthelred, the famous king of the Mercians, there was a noble man of the province of Mercia, who was called Penwald. He was of the oldest and noblest family, who were named Iclings. He was in worldly things wealthy and had great riches, and when he was wealthiest and had the most riches, he desired to take to himself a wife. He chose from the multitude of maidens the one who was fairest, and of the noblest kin; she was called Tette. And they were together until the time that God ordained that the woman became with child. When the time came that she should give birth to the child, suddenly there came a sign from heaven, and clearly as with a seal marked out the child. Lo! men saw a hand of the fairest red hue coming from heaven; and it held a golden rood, and was manifested to many men, and it leaned forward before the door of the house wherein the child was born. Thereupon all the men who saw it hastened thitherward, that they might more clearly see and understand the sign. The hand then returned with the rood up to heaven. Then all the men who saw the sign, stretched themselves on the earth, and prayed God that he would show them what that sign and portent should be, which was there so un-

swá færlice æteowod wæs. Ða hi þa þæt gebed
gefylled heafdon, þa com þær sum wif mid miccle
rædlicnysse yrnan of þam huse þe þæt cild inne
acenned wæs, and cleopode, and cwæð þus to þam
mannum : Bcoð ge staþolfæste and gehyrte, forþan
þæs toweardan wuldres man on þisum middanearde
her ys acenned. Ða hi þa men þæt word gehyrdon,
þa spræcon hig heom betwynan þæt þæt wære god-
cundlic tacn þe þær ætywed wæs, forþon þe þæt bearn
þær acenned wæs. Sume hig þonne cwædon þæt þurh
godcunde stihtunge þære[1] ecan eadignysse him wære
seo gifu forestihtod, þæs haliges tacnes þe him æt
his acennednysse ætywad wæs. Wæron men swiþe
wundriende be þære wisan and be þam tacne þe þær
ætywed wæs : and efne ær þon þe sunne[2] on setl eode
hit wæs ofer eall middel Engla-land cuð and mǽre.

II.

Ða þæs ymbe eahta niht þæs þe mon þæt cild
brohte to þam halgan þwéale fulwihte-bæþes, ða wæs
him nama sceapen of þæs cynnes gereorde and of þære
þeode Guþlac, swa hit wǽre of godcundlicre stihtunge
gedón, þæt he swa genemned wǽre : forþon swá þa
wisan leorneras secgað on Angel-cynne þæt se nama
standeð on twam[3] gewritum : Guðlac se nama ys on
romanisc, Belli múnus : forþon þeah he mid woruld-
lice[4] geswince menige earfoðnysse adreah, and þeah
mid gecyrrednysse þa gife þære ecan eadignysse mid

---

[1] MS. in þære ece. [2] MS. sunna.
[3] MS. feawum. [4] MS. woruldlicre.

expectedly displayed to them. When they had ended this prayer, a woman came in great haste running out of the house wherein the child was born, and said thus to the men: Be firm and of good heart, for a man of future glory is born here on this earth. When the men heard this word, they said among themselves, that it was a divine sign that was there showed to them, inasmuch as the child was born there. Some of them then said, that by divine providence the gift of eternal bliss was fore-ordained to him, in virtue of the holy sign that was shown to them at his birth. Men were much amazed at the matter and at the sign which was there displayed; and behold, ere the sun set it was known and famous over all the middle of England.

II.

About eight nights afterwards, when they brought the child to the holy laver of baptism, a name was given him from the appellation of the family and from the clan, Guthlac, as though it were done by divine providence, that he should be thus named. For thus the wise teachers in England say, that the name consists of two terms; the name Guthlac is in Latin, Belli munus; for that he not only endured many troubles with worldly labour, but also by conversion received the gift of eternal bliss with the

sige eces lifes onfenge, and swá mid þam apostolum
cweþende: Beatus vir qui suffert temptationem; quia
cum probatus fuerit accipiet coronam vite quam repromisit dominus diligentibus sé. þæt ys on englisc:
Eadig man biðe, cwæð he, se þe her on worulde manig-
fealdlice geswincnysse and earfoðnysse dreogeð, forþon mid þam þe he gecostod bið and geswenced,
þonne onfehð he ecum beage; and þæt God gehet
eallum þam þe hine lufiað. After þon þe he wæs
aþwegen mid þam þweale þæs halgan fulluhtes, ða wæs
he eft to þære fæderlican healle gelædd and þær
gefedd. Mid þam þe seo yld com þæt hit sprecan
mihte æfter cniht-wisan, þonne wæs he nawiht hefig,
ne unhyrsum his yldrum on wordum, ne þam þe hine
feddon, nænigum oþþe yldran oþþe gingran. Ne he
cnihtlice galnysse næs begangende, ne idele spel-
lunge folcricra manna, ne úngeliclice olécunge, ne
leaslicetunge: ne he mistlice fugela[1]-sangas ne wur-
þode, swá oft swa cnihtlicu yldo begæð. Ac on his
scearpnysse þæt he weox, and wearð glæd on his
ansyne, and hluttor and clæne on his mode, and bil-
wite on his þeawum. Ac on him wæs se scima
gastlicre beorhtnysse swá swyðe scinende, þæt ealle
þa men þe hine gesawon on him gescon mihton þa
þing þe him towearde wæron. Da wæs æfter sið-
fate þæt mægen on him weox and gestiþode on his
geogoðe, þa gemunde he þa strangan dæda þara un-
manna and þæra woruld-frumena; he þa, swa he of

---

[1] MS. fugelas.

victory of eternal life, saying thus with the apostle :
Beatus vir qui suffert temptationem, quia cum probatus fuerit accipiet coronam vite, quam repromisit
Dominus diligentibus se. That is in English :
Blessed is the man, saith he, who here in the world
endureth manifold labours and troubles, for whereas
he is tempted and tried, then receiveth he the ever-
lasting ~~reward~~ *crown*; and this hath God promised to all
who love him. After he was washed in the laver of
holy baptism, he was led to his father's hall and
there nourished. When the age came that the child
should speak in child-fashion, he was no whit dull,
nor disobedient to his parents in their commands,
nor to those who nurtured him, either elder or
younger. Nor was he addicted to boyish levities,
nor the vain talk of vulgar men, nor unseemly
fawning, nor lying flattery. Nor did he study the
various cries of birds, as childish age is often wont.
But he grew up in sharpness, and was blithe in
countenance, and pure and clean in his disposition,
and innocent in his ways. And in him was the
lustre of divine brightness so shining, that all men
who saw him could perceive in him the promise of
what should hereafter happen to him. After a time,
when his strength waxed and he grew up to man-
hood, then thought he on the strong deeds of the
heroes, and of the men of yore. Then, as though he

slǽpe onwoce, wearð his mod oncyrred, and he
gesomnode miccle scóle and wered his geþoftena
and hys efen-hæfdlingas, and him sylf to wæpnum
feng. Þa wræc he his æfþancas on his feondum,
and heora burh bærnde and heora túnas ofer-
hergode ; and he wide geond eorþan menigfeald
wæl felde and sloh and of mannum heora æhta nam.
þa wæs he semninga innan manod godcundlice and
lǽred þæt he þa word hete, ealle þa he swa [genam]¹
he het þriddan dǽl agifan þam mannum þe he hit
ær ongenǽmde. Da wæs ymbe nigon winter þæs
þe he þa ehtnysse begangende wæs se eadiga
Guthlac, and he hine sylfne betweox þises andweardan middaneardes wealcan dwelode.² þa gelamp
sume nihte³ mid þam þe he com of farendum wege,
and he hys þa werigan lima reste, and he menig
þing mid his mode þohte ; ða wæs he fǽringa mid
Godes ege onbryrd, and mid gastlicre lufan his heorte
innan gefylled : and mid þy he awoc he geþohte þa
ealdan kyningas þe iú wæron,⁴ þurh earmlicne deað
and þurh sarlicne utgang þæs mánfullan lifes, þe
þas woruld forleton ; and þa micclan welan þe hig
ær-hwilon ahton he geseh on hrædlicnysse ealle
gewítan ; and he geseah his agen lif dæghwamlice
to þam ende efstan and scyudan. Ða wæs he
sæmninga mid þam godcundan egesan innan swá
swyþe onbryrded, þæt he audette Gode gif he him
þæs mergen-dæges geunnan wolde, þæt he his þeow

---

¹ [Genam] not in MS.   ² MS. weolc ⁊ welode.   ³ MS. niht.
⁴ MS. and mid þy he geþohte þa caldan kyningas þa iú wæron he
awoc þurh, etc.

had woke from sleep, his disposition was changed, and he collected a great troop and host of his companions and equals, and himself took weapons. Then wreaked he his grudges on his enemies, and burned their city, and ravaged their towns, and widely through the land he made much slaughter, and slew and took from men their goods. Then was he on a sudden inwardly admonished of God, and taught that he should thus give command; of all things which he had so taken he bade give back the third part to those from whom he had taken it. It was about nine years that he was thus engaged in hostile raids, the blessed Guthlac, and he thus wandered amidst the tumult of this present world. It happened on one night when he had come from an expedition, and he rested his weary limbs, and thought over many things in his mind; that he was suddenly inspired with divine awe, and his heart within was filled with spiritual love; and when he awoke, he thought on the old kings who were of yore, who thinking on miserable death, and the wretched end of sinful life, forsook this world; and the great wealth which they once possessed, he saw all on a sudden vanish; and he saw his own life daily hasten and hurry to an end. Then was he suddenly so excited inwardly with godly fear, that he vowed to God, if he would spare him till the morrow, that he would be his servant. When the darkness of

beon wolde. — Mid þy þære nihte þystro gewíton and
hit dæg wæs, þa arás he and hine sylfne getacnode
insegle Cristes rode.   Ða bead he his geferum þæt
hi fundou him oðerne ealdorman and latteow hira
geferscipe; and he him andette and sæde þæt he
wolde beon Cristes þeow.   Mid þam þe his geferan
þas word gehyrdon, þa wæron hi swiþe wundriende,
and swyþe forhte for þam wordum þe hi þær gehyrdon : þa hi ealle to him aluton and hine bǽdon
þæt he næfre þa þing swa gelæste swa he mid
wordum gecwæð.   He þa hwæþere heora worda ne
gimde, ac þæt ilce þæt he ǽr geþohte þæt he þæt
forðlæstan wolde; barn him swá swyþe innan þære
Godes lufan þæt na læs þæt an þæt he þas woruld
forseah, ac swilce hys yldrena gestreon and his eard,
and þa sylfan his heafod-gemacan þæt he þæt eall
forlet.   Ða he wæs feower and twentig wintra eald,
þa forlet he ealle þas woruld-glenga, and eallne his
hiht on Crist gesette : and þa æfter þon þæt he
ferde to mynstre þe ys gecweden Hrypadún, and
þær þa gerynelican sceare onfeng, Sce Petres
þæs apostoles under Ælfðryðe abbodyssan : and
syþþan he to sceare and to þam munuc-life feng,
hwæt he nænigre wætan onbítan nolde þe drun-
cennys [1] þurh cóme.   And þa for þan þingum hine
þa broðra hatedon, þy he swá forhæbbende wæs :
and þa raðe syþþan hi þa hluttorlicnysse his modes,
and þa clænnysse his lifes ongéaton, þæt hig ealle

---

[1] MS. druncennysse.

night was gone, and it was day, he arose and signed himself with the mark of Christ's rood. Then bade he his companions that they should find them another captain and leader of their company; and he confessed to them, and said that he would be Christ's servant. When his companions heard these words, they were greatly astonished, and very alarmed for the words which they had heard. Then they all bowed to him, and begged him that he never would perform the things which he had in words expressed. He however cared not for their words, but the same thing that he had first intended, that would he perform. God's love burnt so within him, that not only did he despise this world, but also his parents' wealth and his home, and even his companions he all forsook. When he was four and twenty years old, he forsook all the pomps of the world, and set all his hope on Christ. And after that he went to a monastery, which is called Hrypadun, and there received the mystical tonsure of St. Peter the apostle, under abbess Ælfthrytha. And after he had taken the tonsure and the monastic life, lo! he would taste no liquid through which drunkenness comes. And for these things the brethren hated him, because he was so abstinent; but soon after, when they perceived the purity of his mind, and the cleanness of his life, they all loved him. He was in

hine lufedon. Wæs he on ansine mycel and on
lichaman clǽne, wynsum on his mode, and wlitig
on ansyne; he wæs liðe and gemetfæst on his
worde, and he wæs geþyldig and eadmod; and á seo
godcunde lufu on hys heortan hat and byrnende.
Mid þy he þa wæs in stafas and on leornunge ge-
togen, þa girnde he his sealmas to leornianne: þa
wǽron þa wæstm-berendan breost þæs eadigan weres
mid Godes gife gefyllede and mid þam lareowdóme
þæs hean magistres Godes, þæt he wæs on godcund-
lican þeodscipe getyd and gelæred. Mid þam þe
he wæs twa gear on þære leornunge, ða hæfde he
his sealmas geleornod and canticas, and ymnas, and
gebeda æfter cyriclicre endebyrdnysse. þa ongan
he wurðigan þa gódan þeawas þara godra on þam life,
eadnysse,[1] and hyrsumnysse, geþyld, and þolemod-
nysse, and forhæfednysse his lichaman; and ealra
þara godra mægen he wæs begangende. Ða ymbe twá
winter þæs þe he his lif swá leofode under munuchade þæt he þa ongan wilnian westenes and sunder-
setle. Mid þy he gehyrde secgan and he leornode
be þam ancerum, þe geara on westene and on sundor-
settlum for Godes naman wilnodon and heora lif
leofodon, ða wæs his heorte innan þurh Godes gifu
onbryrdod, þæt he westenes gewilnode. Ða wæs
sona ymbe unmanige dagas þæt he him leafe bæd æt
þam þeowum þe þǽr yldest wǽron þæt he féran moste.

---

[1] Perhaps a mistake for eadmodnysse.

figure tall, and pure in body, cheerful in mood, and in countenance handsome ; he was mild and modest in his discourse, and he was patient and humble ; and ever in his heart was divine love hot and burning. When he devoted himself to letters and learning, he was desirous of learning his psalms. Then was the fruitful breast of the blessed man filled with God's grace, and with the teaching of God the great master he became instructed and learned in divine discipline. When he had been two years on this study, he had learned his psalms, and canticles, and hymns, and prayers, after ecclesiastical order. Then began he to study the good observances of the virtuous in that life, gentleness and obedience, patience and long suffering, and abstinence of body ; and he cultivated the virtues of all good men. After he had passed about two years of his life thus in the monastic state, he began to long for the wilderness and a hermitage. When he heard tell and learned concerning anchorites who of yore longed for the wilderness and hermitages for God's name, and passed their lives there, his heart was inwardly inspired with the love of God to long for the wilderness. So then not many days after, he begged leave from the servants [of God] who were the eldest there, that he might depart.

III.

Ys on Bretonc-lande sum fenn unmætre mycel-
nysse þæt onginneð fram Grante eá naht feor
fram þære cestre, ðy ylcan nama ys nemned Grante-
ceaster. þær synd unmæte[1] moras, hwilon sweart
wæter-steal, and hwilon fúle éa-riþas yrnende, and
swylce eac manige ealand and hreod and beorhgas
and treow-gewrido, and hit mid menigfealdan bignyssum widgille and lang þurhwunað[2] on norð-sǽ.
Mid þan se foresprecena wer and þære eadigan
gemynde Guðlac[3] þæs wídgillan westenes þa ungear-
awan stowe þær gemette, þa wæs he mid godcunde[4]
fultume gefylst, and þa sona þan rihtestan wege þyder
togeferde. þa wæs mid þam þe he þyder com þæt he
frægn þa bigengcan þæs landes, hwær he on þam
westene him eardung-stowe findan mihte. Mid þy
hi him menigfeald þing sædon be þære wídgilnysse
þæs westenes. Þa wæs Tátwine gehaten sum man,
sǽde þa þæt he wiste sum ealand synderlice digle,
þæt oft menige men eardian ongunnon, ac for menig-
fealdum brogum and egsum, and for annysse þæs
widgillan westenes þæt hit nænig man adreogan ne
mihte, ac hit ælc forþan befluge. Mid þam þe se
halga wer Guðlac þa word gehyrde, he bæd sona þæt
he him þa stowe getæhte, and he þa sona swa dyde ;
code þa on scip, and þa ferdon begen þurh þa rugan
fennas oþ þæt hi comon to þære stowe þe man hateð

---

[1] MS. unmæetre.   [2] MS þeneð wunað.
[3] MS. Guðlaces.   [4] MS. godcundre.

III.

There is in Britain a fen of immense size, which begins from the river Granta not far from the city, which is named Grantchester. There are immense marshes, now a black pool of water, now foul running streams, and also many islands, and reeds, and hillocks, and thickets, and with manifold windings wide and long it continues up to the north sea. When the aforesaid man, Guthlac of blessed memory, found out this uncultivated spot of the wide wilderness, he was comforted with divine support, and journeyed forthwith by the straightest way thither. And when he came there he inquired of the inhabitants of the land where he might find himself a dwelling-place in the wilderness. Whereupon they told him many things about the vastness of the wilderness. There was a man named Tatwine, who said that he knew an island especially obscure, which ofttimes many men had attempted to inhabit, but no man could do it on account of manifold horrors and fears, and the loneliness of the wide wilderness; so that no man could endure it, but every one on this account had fled from it. When the holy man Guthlac heard these words, he bid him straightway show him the place, and he did so; he embarked in a vessel, and they went both through the wild fens till they came to the spot which is called Crowland;

Cruwland : wæs þæt land on middan þam westene
swá gerád geseted þæs foresædan fennes,[1] swyðe
digle, and hit swyþe feawa[2] men wiston buton þam
anum þe hyt him tæhte ; swylc þær næfre nænig
man ǽr eardian ne mihte ær se eadiga wer Guðlac to-
com for þære eardunga þara awerigedra gasta.   And
he þa se eadiga wer Guðlac forhogode sona þa
costunge þæra awerigdra gasta, and mid heofonlicum
fultume gestrangod weard, betwyx þa fenlican
gewrido þæs widgillan westenes, þæt he ana ongan
eardian.   Ða gelamp mid þære godcundan stihtunge,
þæt he on þa tid Sce Bartholomei þæs apostoles þæt
he com to þam ealande, forþan he on eallum þingum
his fultum sohte.   And he þa gelufode þære[3] stowe
digelnysse, and he þa gehet þæt he wolde ealle dagas
his lifes þær on þam ealande Gode þeowian. Mid þy
he þa unmanige dagas þær wæs, þa geondsceawode he
þa þing þe to þære stowe belumpon.   Ða þohte he
þæt.he eft wolde to þam mynstre feran and his ge-
broðra gretan, forþan he ær fram heom ungegret
gewat.   Ða þæs on mergen mid þan hit dæg wæs
þa ferde he eft to þam mynstre ; þa wæs he þær
hundnigantig nihta mid þam broðrum : and þa syþþan
he hig grette, he þa eft hwærf to þære stowe þæs
leofan westenes mid twam cnihtum. Ða wæs se
eahtoða dæg þæs kalendes Septembres, þe man on
þa tid wurðað Sce Bartholomei þæs apostoles, þa se
eadiga wer Guðlac com to þære foresprecenan stowe,

---

[1] MS. fennas.   [2] MS. feawe.   [3] MS. þa.

this land was in such wise (as he said) situated in the midst of the waste of the aforesaid fen, very obscure, and very few men knew of it except the one who showed it to him ; as no man ever could inhabit it before the holy man Guthlac came thither, on account of the dwelling of the accursed spirits there. And the blessed man Guthlac disregarded the temptation of the accursed spirits, and was strengthened with heavenly support, so that he began to dwell alone among the fenny thickets of the wide wilderness. It fell out, by divine providence, that he came to the island on the day of St. Bartholomew the apostle ; for he sought in all things his support. And he was enamoured of the obscurity of the place, and vowed that he would serve God on that island all the days of his life. When he had been there not many days, he looked about at the things which appertained to the place. Then he thought that he would return again to the monastery, and salute his brethren, for he had before gone away from them without taking leave. So in the morning, when it was day, he went back to the monastery ; there he remained with the brethren ninety nights. And after he had taken leave of them, he returned back again to the place of his beloved wilderness with two servants. It was the eighth day before the kalends of September, which is observed as the day of St. Bartholomew the apostle, when the holy man Guthlac

to Cruwlande, forþon he his fultum on eallum þingum
ærest to þam sundor-setle sohte.   Hæfde he þa on
ylde six and twentig wintra þa he ærest se Godes
cempa on þam westene mid heofenlicre gife geweorðod
gesæt.[1]   Þa sona wið þam scotungum þara werigra
gasta þæt he hine mid gastlicum wæpnum gescylde,
he nam þone scyld þæs Halgan Gastes geleafan ; and
hyne on þære byrnan gegearowode þæs heofonlican
hihtes; and he him dyde heolm on heafod clænera[2]
geþanca ; and mid þam strǽlum þæs halgan sealm-
sanges[3] á singallice wið þam awerigedum gastum
sceotode and campode.   And nu hwæt ys swa swiþe
to wundrianne þa diglan mihte ures Drihtnes, and
his mildheortnysse domas;   hwa mæg þa ealle
asecgan ! Swá se æþela lareow ealra þeoda Scs Paulus
se apostol, þone ure Drihten ælmihtig God fore-
stihtode to godspellianne his folce; he wæs ǽr-þon
ehtere his þære halgan cyrcan, and mid þan þe he
tó Damascum ferde þære byrig, þæt he wæs of þam
þystrum gedwolum abroden Iudea ungeleafulnysse
mid þam swege heofonlicre stefne ; swá þonne þære
arwurðan gemynde Guðlac of þære gedrefednysse
þissere worulde wæs gelǽded to campháde þæs ecan
lifes.

---

[1] MS. geweorðod.   Gesæt þa.   [2] MS. clænere.
[3] MS. sealm-sangas.

came to the aforesaid place Crowland, for that he sought his support first in all things in regard to his solitary life. He was six and twenty years of age when, endowed with heavenly grace, God's soldier first settled in the wilderness. Then straightway, that he might arm himself against the attacks of the wicked spirits with spiritual weapons, he took the shield of the Holy Spirit, faith; and clothed himself in the armour of heavenly hope; and put on his head the helmet of chaste thoughts; and with the arrows of holy psalmody he ever continually shot and fought against the accursed spirits. And now how greatly must we admire the secret might of our Lord, and the judgments of his mercy; who can tell them all? As the noble teacher of all nations, St. Paul the apostle, whom our Lord Almighty God fore-appointed to preach the gospel to his people; he was before a persecutor of his holy church, and whilst he journeyed to the city Damascus he was delivered from the dark errors of the Jews' unbelief by the sound of a heavenly voice; so Guthlac of venerated memory was led from the tribulation of this world to the victory of eternal life.

IV.

Be þam halgan were hu he eardode on þǽre stówe.

XXVIII Onginne ic nu be ðam life ðæs eadigan weres Guðlaces, swa swa ic gehyrde secgan þa þe his lif cuðon, Wilfrid and Cissa; þonne secge ic swá æfter þære endebyrdnysse. Wæs þær on þam ealande sum hlaw mycel ofer eorðan geworht, þone ylcan men iú geara for feos wilnunga gedulfon and brǽcon. þa wæs þær on oþre sidan þæs hlawes[1] gedolfen swylce mycel wæter-seað wǽre. On þam seaðe ufan se eadiga wer Guthlac him hus getimbrode, sona fram fruman þæs þe he þæt ancer-setl[2] gesæt. þa geþohte he þæt he naðor ne wyllenes hrægles ne linenes brucan nolde, ac on fellenum gegyrelan þæt he wolde ealle his dagas his lifes alifian; and he hit swá forð-gelæstende wæs. Ælce dǽge wæs his bigleofan swylc gemetegung[3] of þære tide þe he þæt westen eardigan ongan, þæt he nawiht ne onbyrigde buton berenne[4] hlaf and wæter; and þonne sunne wæs on setle, þonne þigede he þa[5] andlyfene þe he bigleofode. Sona þæs þe he westen eardigan ongan, þa gelamp hit sume dæge mid [þy he][6] þan gewune-lican þeawe his sealm sang and his gebedum befeal, þa se ealda feond man-cynnes (efne swa grymetigende leo, þæt he his costunga attor wide todæleð,) mid þy he þa his yfelnysse mǽgen and grymnysse attor

---

[1] MS. hlawas.   [2] MS. ancer-setle.   [3] MS. to gereorde.
[4] MS. berene.   [5] MS. þæs.   [6] [þy he] not in MS.

IV.

Concerning the holy man, how he dwelt in the place.

I begin now to speak of the life of the blessed man Guthlac, as I have heard those relate who knew his life, Wilfrid and Cissa; and according thereto I tell it in order. There was on the island a great mound raised upon the earth, which same of yore men had dug and broken up in hopes of treasure. On the other side of the mound a place was dug, as it were a great water-cistern. Over this cistern the blessed man Guthlac built himself a house at the beginning, as soon as he settled in the hermit-station. Then he resolved that he would use neither woollen nor linen garment, but that he would live all the days of his life in clothing of skins; and so he continued to do. Each day, from the time that he began to dwell in the wilderness, the abstemiousness of his diet was such, that he never tasted aught but barley-bread and water; and when the sun was set, then took he his food on which he lived. Soon after he began to dwell in the wilderness, it happened one day, when he had, after his wonted custom, sung a psalm and fell to his prayers, that the old enemy of mankind (who, even as a roaring lion, scatters wide the venom of his temptations), whilst he [was scattering abroad] the might of his

[todælde]¹ þæt he mid þan þa menniscan heortan
wundode, þa semninga swá he of gebendum bogan
his costunge streale on þam mode gefæstnode þæs
Cristes cempan. Ða he þa se eadiga wer mid þære
geættredan streale gewundod wǽs þæs awerigedan
gastes, ꝺa wæs his mod þæs eadigan weres swiꝺe
gedrefed on him, be þam onginne þe he ongan þæt
westen swá ana eardigan. Mid þam he þa hine
hider and þyder gelomlice on his mode cyrde, and
gemunde þa ǽrran synna and leahtras þe he gefre-
mede and geworht hæfde, and þa máran and un-
mǽttran² him sylfa dyde þonne he wende þæt he hi
æfre gebetan mihte. Ða hæfde hine seo deofollice
strǽl mid ormodnysse gewundodne : wæs se eadiga
wer Guꝺlac mid þære ormodnysse þri dagas gewundod, þæt he sylfa nyste hwider he wolde mid
his móde gecyrran. Ða wæs py þryddan dǽge þære
æfter-fylgendan nihte þæt he þam tweogendum
geþohtum fæstlice wiꝺstód ; and efne swá witedomlice muþe þæt he sang and clypode to Gode, and
cwæꝺ : In tribulatione mea invocavi Ðominum, et
reliqua. þæt ys on englisc : Min Drihten on minre
geswincnysse ic þe to clypige, ac gehyr þu me and
gefultuma me on minum earfeꝺum. Ða wæs sona
æfter þon þæt his se getreowa fultum him to com,
Scs Bartholomeus ; and na læs þæt he him on slǽpe
ætywde, ac he wæccende þone apostol on engellicre
fægernysse geseah and sceawode. And he þa sona

¹ [todælde] not in MS.   ² MS. unmǽttra.

wickedness and the venom of his cruelty, that he might wound the hearts of men therewith, suddenly, as from a bended bow, he fixed the dart of his temptation in the soul of Christ's soldier. When, therefore, the blessed man was wounded with the poisoned arrow of the accursed spirit, his soul (the blessed man's) was greatly troubled within him, about the undertaking he had begun, namely, to dwell thus alone in the wilderness. Then he turned himself hither and thither continually in his mind, and thought of his former sins and wickednesses which he had committed and wrought, and how that he himself had done greater and more enormous sins than he thought he could ever compensate for. Thus had the devilish arrow wounded him with desperation: the blessed man Guthlac was three days wounded with this despair, so that he himself knew not whither he would turn with his thoughts. It was upon the night following the third day that he firmly withstood these doubting thoughts; and thereupon with prophetic mouth he sang and cried to God, and said: In tribulatione meâ invocavi Ðominum, et reliqua. That is, in English: My Lord, in my trouble I cry unto thee, and hear thou me, and support me in my tribulations. It was soon after this that his faithful support, St. Bartholomew, came to him, and did not appear to him in sleep, but waking he saw and beheld the apostle in angelic beauty.

se eadiga wer Guðlac swyþe bliþe wæs þæs heofonlican cuman; and him sona his heorte and his
geþanc call wæs onlihtod; and he þa hrædlice þa
yfelan and þa twyfcaldan geþohtas forlet, and hine
se heofonlica cuma frefrode, Scs Bartholomeus, and
hine mid wordum trymede and strangode, and hine
het þæt he ne tweode, ac þæt he wǽre ánrǽd; and
þæt he him on fultume beon wolde on eallum his
earfeðum.   Ða se halga Guðlac þas word gehyrde
his þæs getreowan freondes, þa wæs he mid gastlicre
blisse gefylled, and his geleafan fæste on God sylfne
getrymede and fæstnode.

V.

Swylce eac gelamp on sumne sæl, mid þy he be
þære drohtnunge smeade his lifes, hu he Gode
gecwemlicost mihte lybban, ða comon semninga
twegen deoflu to him of þære lyfte slidan and þa to
him cuðlice spræcon and cwædon: We syndon
gewisse þines lifes, and þines geleafan trumnesse
we witon, and eac þin geþyld we cunnon únofer-
swyþed; and þær we þin fandedon, and costodon,
þæt we mid manigfealde cræfte úre[1] wǽpna wið þe
sendon.   We nu heonon-forð nellað þe leng swencan
ne þe bysmrian; na læs þæt an þæt we þe þæs nu
nellað lettan þæs þu ær geþoht hæfdest, ac we þe
eac wyllað secgan be þam eallum þe iu geara westen[2]

---

[1] MS. úra.   [2] MS. westene.

And forthwith the blessed man Guthlac was right glad of the heavenly visitor; and his heart and mind was soon all enlightened, and he quickly let go the bad and desperate thoughts; and the heavenly visitor, St. Bartholomew, comforted him, and confirmed and strengthened him with his words, and bid him not despair, but be constant; and said that he would be his support in all his tribulations. When the holy Guthlac heard these words of his faithful friend, he was filled with spiritual joy, and strengthened and fixed his faith firmly upon God himself.

V.

It happened, also, on one occasion, when he was reflecting upon the conduct of his life, how he might live most acceptably to God, there came suddenly two devils to him, sliding down from the air, and they spoke plainly to him, and said: We are acquainted with thy life, and the firmness of thy faith we know, and also we know thy patience to be unconquered; and therein we tried and proved thee, whilst with manifold craft we directed our weapons at thee. We now henceforth will no longer trouble nor injure thee; not only will we now cease to hinder thee from that which thou didst first intend, but we will even tell thee respecting all those who of yore inhabited the wilderness, how they lived

eardedon, hu hi heora lif leofodon. Moyses ærest
and Helias hi fæston, and swylce eac se Hælend
ealles middaneardes on westene he fæste, and eac
swylce þa mǽran munecas þa mid Ægiptum wæron
and þǽr on westenum wunedon : þa þurh heora forhæfdnysse on heom ealle uncyste ofaslógon and
ácwealdon.   Þonne gif þu þæt wilnast þæt þu of þe
þa ǽr gefremedan synna aþwéan wylt, þonne scealt
þu þinne lichaman þurh forhæfdnysse wæccan; forþon
swá myccle swa þu þe her on worulde swyþor swincst,
swá þu eft byst on ecnysse fæstlicor getrymed ; and
swá myccle swá þu on þisum andweardan life má
earfoða drigast, swá myccle þu eft on toweardnysse
gefehst ; and þonne þu on fæsten her on worulde
gestihst, þonne bist þu ahafen for Godes eagum.
Forþon þin fæsten ne sccal beon þæt an twegra
daga fyrst oþþe þreora oþþe ǽlce dǽge, þæt þu þe
swá on[1] tela myccle forhæfdnysse ahebbe, ac on
seofon nihta fyrstes fæstene biþ to clǽnsienne þone
man.   Swá on six dagum ærest God ealles middan-
cardes fægernysse gehiwode and gefrætwode, and on
þam seofoþan he hinc reste, swa þonne gedafenað
þam þe gelice þurh six daga fæsten þone gast
gefrætwian, and þonne þy seofoðan dæge[2] mete
þicgan and þonc[3] lichaman restan.   Ða se eadiga
wer Guðlac þas word gehyrde, þa aras he sona and
to Gode clypode, and hyne gebæd and þus cwæð :
Syn mine fynd, min Drihten God, á on-hinder ge-

<hr />

[1] MS. on swá.   [2] MS. dæg.   [3] MS. his.

their lives. Moses first, and Elijah, they fasted, and also the Saviour of all the earth, he fasted in the wilderness; and also the famous monks who were in Egypt and dwelt there in deserts; they, through their abstinence, slew and quelled in themselves all corruption. Therefore, if thou desirest to wash from thee the sins thou didst once commit, thou shouldst afflict thy body with abstinence; because by how much the more severely thou afflictest thyself in this world, by so much the more firmly shalt thou be strengthened to eternity; and by how much thou sufferest more troubles in this present life, so much the more shalt thou receive in future; and when thou advancest here in the world in fasting, thou shalt then be exalted in God's eyes. Therefore thy fasting must not be a space of two or three days, nor on each day, that thou shouldst exalt thyself thereupon as a very great abstinence, but it is necessary by a fast of seven nights' duration to cleanse the man. As on six days God first formed and adorned the beauty of the whole earth, and on the seventh rested himself; so, also, beseems it thee in like manner by six days' fast to adorn the spirit, and then on the seventh day to take meat and to rest the body. When the blessed man Guthlac heard these words, he arose and cried to God, and prayed, and thus said: Let my foes, my Lord God,

2 §

cyrde, forþon ic þe ongite and oncnawe, forþon þe
þu eart min scyppend.   þa sona æfter þam wordum
se awyrigeda gast efne swá smic beforan his ansyne
áidlode.   He þa forseah þa deofollican láre, for þam
þe he ealle þa ydele ongeat; ac þa feng [to][1] méd-
mycclan bigleofan, þæt wæs to þam berenan hláfe,
and þone þigede and his lif bileofode.   Ða þa
awyrigedan gastas þæt ongeaton þæt he hig ealle
forhógode and heora lara, hig þa þæt mid wependre
stefne sorhgodon, þæt hi oferswiðde wǽron; and
se eadiga wer swá gesigefæstod wearð þæt he þa
bysmornysse forhogode heora lára and heora costunga.
Swylce eac gelámp on sumne.sǽl ymb únmanige
dagas þæt he wæccende þa niht on halgum gebedum
awunode.   Þa on þære nihte stilnysse gelamp
semninga, þæt þær comon mycele meniu þara
awyrigedra gasta, and hi eall þæt hus mid heora
cyme fyldon; and hi on ealce healfe inguton ufan
and neoðan and eghwonen. Hi wǽron on ansyne
egslice and big hæfdon mycele heafda, and laugne
sweoran, and mægere[2] ansyne : hi wǽron fúlice and
orfyrme on heora beardum; and hi hæfdon[3] ruge
earan, and woh nebb and reðelice eagan, and fúle
muðas; and heora toþas wǽron gelíce horses twuxan;
and him wǽron þa þrotan mid lege gefylde, and
hi wǽron ongristlice on stefne : hi hæfdon woge
sceancan, and mycele cneowu and hindan greate,

---

[1] [to] not in MS.   [2] MS. manigre.
[3] MS. and ruge earan and hi hæfdon woh nebb.

be for ever turned backwards, for I know and understand thee, that thou art my Maker. Immediately
after these words the accursed spirit vanished from
before his face like smoke. Then despised he the
devilish doctrine, for he understood that it was all
vain; and he took a moderate meal, that is, the
barley loaf, and ate it, and supported his life. When
the cursed spirits understood that he despised them
all, and their doctrines, they bewailed with lament-
able voice that they were overcome; and the blessed
man was so victorious that he despised the blas-
phemies of their doctrines and of their temptations.
Also it happened, on a time not many days after,
that he was passing the night waking in holy prayers.
Then in the stillness of the night it happened
suddenly that there came great hosts of the accursed
spirits, and they filled all the house with their
coming; and they poured in on every side, from
above and from beneath, and everywhere. They
were in countenance horrible, and they had great
heads, and a long neck, and lean visage; they were
filthy and squalid in their beards; and they had
rough ears, and distorted face, and fierce eyes, and
foul mouths; and their teeth were like horses' tusks;
and their throats were filled with flame, and they
were grating in their voice; they had crooked
shanks, and knees big and great behind, and dis-

and misscrence tán,[1] and hás hrymedon on[2] stefnum ;
and hi þa swá ungemetlicum[3] gestundum foron and
swá unmetlice[4] ege, þæt him þuhte þæt hit eall
betweox heofone and eorðan hleoþrode þam eges-
licum stefnum.   Næs þa nænig yldend to þam þæt
syþþan hi on þæt hus comon hi þa sona þone halgan
wer eallum limum gebundon, and hi hine tugon
and læddon ut of þære cytan, and hine þa læddon
on þone sweartan fenn and hine þa on þa horwihtan[5]
wæter bewurpon and besencton.   Æfter þon hi
hine lǽddon on þam reðum stowum þæs westenes,
betwux þa þiccan gewrido þara bremela þæt him
wæs call se lichama gewundod.   Mid þy hi þa lange
on þære þystrunge hine swa swencton, þa léton hi
hine ane hwíle abidan and gestandan ;   heton hine þa
þæt he of þam westene gewite, oþþe gif he þæt
nolde, þonne woldon hi hine mid máran bysmerum
swencan and costian.   He þa se eadiga wer Guðlac
heora worda ne gimde, ac he mid witegiende muðe
þus cwæð : Drihten me ys on þa swyþran healfe, forþon ic ne beo oncyrred fram þe.   Ða æfter þan þa
awerigedan gastas hine genamon and hine swungon
mid isenum swipum, and þa æfter þon hi hine
læddon on þam ongryrlican fiðerum betwux þa
cealdan faca þære lyfte.   þa he þa wæs on þære
heannysse þære lyfte, þa geseah he ealne norð-dǽl
heofones, swylce he wǽre þam sweartestan wolcnum
ymbseald swiðlicra þeostra.   Ða geseah he fǽringa

---

[1] MS. mís crocetton.   [2] hás runigendum stefnum.
[3] MS. ungemetlicre.   [4] MS. unmetlicre.   [5] MS. orwehtan.

torted toes, and shrieked hoarsely with their voices; and they came with such immoderate noises and immense horror, that it seemed to him that all between heaven and earth resounded with their dreadful cries. Without delay, when they were come into the house, they soon bound the holy man in all his limbs, and they pulled and led him out of the cottage, and brought him to the black fen, and threw and sunk him in the muddy waters. After that they brought him to the wild places of the wilderness, among the dense thickets of brambles, that all his body was torn. After they had a long time thus tormented him in darkness, they let him abide and stand a while; then commanded him to depart from the wilderness, or if he would not do so, then they would torment and try him with greater plagues. He, the blessed man Guthlac, cared not for their words, but with prophetic mouth he thus spake: The Lord is on my right hand, that I be not turned back from thee. After that the cursed spirits took him and beat him with iron whips, and after that they brought him on their creaking wings amidst the cold regions of the air. When he was at this height in the air he saw all the north part of heaven as it were surrounded by the blackest clouds of intense darkness. Then he saw suddenly

unmǽtc[1] werod þæra awerigedra gasta him ongean
cuman; and hi þa sona þær tosomne gegaderodon, and
hi þa sona ealle þone halgan wer gelǽddon to þam
sweartum tintreh-stowum, helle dura[2] hi hine
gebrohton.   Ða he þa þær gesceah þa fulnysse þæs
smyces and þa byrnendan[3] lega and þone ege þære
sweartan deopnysse, he þa sona wæs forgitende ealra
þara tintrega and þæra wita þe he fram þam awyr-
gedum gastum ǽr dreah and áþolode.   Hi þa sona
þa awyrgedan gastas betwux þa grimlican lega[4]
inhruron and feollon, and þær þara árleasra manna
sawla mid manigfealdum wítum getintregodon.
Ða se eadiga Guthlac þa micelnysse geseah þara
wita,[5] þa wæs he for þæra egsan swyðe afyrht.   Ða
cleopodon sona þa awyrgedan gastas mid mycelre
cleopunge and þus cwǽdon : Us ys miht geseald þe
to sceofanne on þas witu þisse deopnysse, and her
[is][6] þæt fyr þæt þu sylfa on þe onbǽrndest ; and
for þinum synnum and gyltum helle duru þe ongean
openað.   Mid py þa awyrgedan gastas þisum wordum
béotodon, ða andswerode he heom þus, and cwæð :
Wá eow þeostra bearn and forwyrde tudder,[7] ge
syndon dust and acsan and ysela : hwa scalde eow
earman þæt ge min ahton geweald on þas witu to
sendanne? hwæt ic her eom andweard and gearn,
and bidige nimes Drihtnes willan ; for hwon sceolon
ge mid eowrum leasum beotingum me egsian ? Hig

---

[1] MS. nnmæta.   [2] MS. duru.   [3] MS. byrnenda.   [4] MS. lege.
     [5] MS. wítu.   [6] [is] not in MS.   [7] MS. tuddre.

an immense host of cursed spirits come towards him;
and they soon gathered together, and forthwith all
led the holy man to the black places of torment,
and brought him to hell's door. When he saw
the foulness of the smoke and the burning flames,
and the horror of the black abyss, he quickly forgot
all the torments and the punishments which he had
before suffered and endured from the accursed spirits.
Then the cursed spirits rushed in and tumbled
among the horrible flames, and there they tormented
with manifold punishments the souls of unrighteous
men. When the blessed Guthlac saw the greatness
of the punishments, he was much terrified for dread
of them. Then cried the cursed spirits with a great
voice and thus spake: Power is given us to thrust
thee into the torments of this abyss; and here is
the fire which thou thyself didst kindle within thee,
and for thy sins and crimes hell's door openeth before thee. When the accursed spirits had threatened
him with these words, then answered he them thus,
and said: Woe to you! children of darkness, and
seed of destruction; ye are dust and cinders and
ashes; who granted you, wretches, that ye should
have power over me, to send me to these punishments! Lo! I am here present and ready, and await
my Lord's will; wherefore should ye frighten me
with your false threats? They then, the accursed

þa sona þa awyrgedan gastas[1] to þam eadigan
woldon swylce hi hine þǽr insceofan woldon. Ða
semninga com se heofones bigengca se halga apostol
Scs Bartholomeus, mid heofonlicre byrhtnysse and
wuldre scinende, betwuhx þa dimnysse þeostru þǽre
sweartan helle.   Hi þa awyrgedan gastas ne mihton
for þære fǽgernysse þæs halgan cuman þǽr awunian,
ac hi sylfe on þeostre gehyddon.   Ða se eadiga wer
Guthlac his þone getreowan freond geseah, þa wæs
he mid gastlicre blisse and mid heofonlice[2] gefean
swiðe bliþe.   Ða æfter þam het se halga apostol ·
Scs Bartholomeus and heom behead þæt hi him
wǽron underþeodde, þæt hi hine eft gebrohton mid
smyltnysse on þære ylcan stowe þe hi hine ær æt-
genamon : and hig þa swá dydon, and hine mid
ealre smyltnysse swá gelæddon, and on heora fiðerum
bǽron and feredon, þæt he ne mihte ne on scipe
fægeror gefered beon.   Mid þy hi þa comon on
middan þære lyfte heannysse, ða comon him togeanes
haligra gasta heap, and hi ealle sungon and þus
cwædon : Ibnut de virtute in virtutem, et reliqua.
Ðæt ys on englisc : Halige men gangeð of mægene
on mægen.   Ða hit þa on mergen dagian wolde þa
asetton hi hine eft þær hi hine ǽr genamon.[3]   Ða
he þa his morgen-gebed-tida wolde Gode gefyllan,
þa geseah he þær standan twegen þara awerigdra
gasta wepan[4] swyþe and geomerian.   Mid þy he hi
ahsode for hwan hi weopon, þa andswarodon hi him

---

[1] MS. gastes.   [2] MS. heofonlicre.   [3] MS. genaman.   [4] MS. weopon.

spirits, motioned towards the blessed man as though they would push him in. There suddenly came the inhabitant of heaven, the holy apostle St. Bartholomew, shining with heavenly brightness and glory, amidst the dim darkness of the black hell. The accursed spirits were not able to abide there for the splendour of the holy visitor, but they hid themselves in the darkness. When the blessed man Guthlac saw his faithful friend he was greatly rejoiced with spiritual gladness and heavenly joy. After this the holy apostle St. Bartholomew bade and commanded them that they should be subject to him, and that they should bring him again with gentleness to the same place which they had before taken him from. And they did so, and brought him with all gentleness and care, and carried him on their wings, that he could not have been carried more pleasantly in a boat. When they came in the midst of the height of the air, there came towards him a troop of holy spirits, and they all sung and spake thus: Ibnut de virtute in virtutem, et reliqua. That is in English: Holy men shall go from virtue to virtue. When it began to dawn in the morning they set him again in the place whence they had taken him. When he then was about to perform his morning prayers to God, he saw two of the cursed spirits standing there weeping and wailing greatly. When he asked them why they wept, they answered

and þus cwædon : Wit wepað forþon þe uncer mægn
eall þurh þe ys gebrocen, and we þe nu ne moton to
cuman, ne to þe nane spræce habban ; ac on eallum
þingum þu unc hæfst gebysmrod, and ure miht eall
oferswyþed. Ða æfter þam wordum hi gewiton ða
awyrgedan gastas[1] efne swá smic fram his ansyne.

VI.

Hu þa deofla on brytisc spræcon.

Ðæt gelamp on þam dagum Cenredes Mercna
kyninges, þæt Brytta-þeod Angol-cynnes feond þæt
hi mid manigum gewinnum and mid missenlicum
gefeohtum þæt hi Angol-cynne geswencton. Ða
gelamp hit sumre nihte þa hit wæs hancred, and se
eadiga wer Guðlac his uht-gebedum befeal, þa wæs
he sæmninga mid leohte slæpe swefed. þa onbræd
he Guðlac of þam slæpe, and eode þa sona út and
hawode and hercnode ; þa gehyrde he mycel werod
þara awyrgedra gasta on bryttisc sprecende ; and
he oncncow and ongeat heora gereorda for þam he
ær hwilon mid him wæs on wráce. Ða sona æfter
þon he geseah eall his hus mid fyre afylled, and hi
hine æfter þon ealne mid spera ordum afyldon, and
hi hine on þam sperum up on þa lyft áhengon. þa
ongeat sona se stranga Cristes cempa þæt þæt wæron
þa egsan and þa witu þæs awyrgedan gastes ; he þa
sona unforhtlice þa stræle þara awerigdra gasta him

---

[1] MS. gastes.

him, and spake thus: We two weep because our power is all broken through thee, and we now may not come at thee, nor have any speech with thee; but in all things thou hast injured us, and altogether overcome our might. After those words the accursed spirits departed, even as smoke, from his face.

VI.

How the devils spake in British.

It happened in the days of Cenred, king of the Mercians, that the British nation, the enemy of the Angle race, with many battles and various contests annoyed the English. It happened one night, when it was the time of cock-crowing, and the blessed man Guthlac fell to his morning prayers, he was suddenly entranced in light slumber. Then Guthlac woke from his sleep, and went immediately out and looked and hearkened; there he heard a great host of the accursed spirits speaking in British; and he knew and understood their words, because he had been erewhile in exile among them. Soon after that he saw all his house filled with fire, and they next struck him quite down with the points of spears, and hung him up in the air on the spears. Then understood the strong warrior of Christ that these were the terrors and the torments of the cursed spirits; he then soon fearlessly thrust from

fram asceaf, and þone sealm sang: Exurgat deus
et dissipentur, et reliqua.　Sona swá he þæt
fyrmeste fers sang þæs sealmes, þa gewiton hi swa
swa smíc fram his ansyne.[35] Mid þy se eadiga wer
Guðlac swa gelomlice wið þam awerigedum gastum
wann and campode, þa ongeaton hi þæt heora mægn
and weorc oferswyþed wæs.

VII.

Be Beccelle þam preoste.

Wæs sum preost þæs nama wæs Beccel; þa com
he to þam halgan were, and hine bæd þæt he hine
to him genáme, and þæt gehet þæt he eadmodlice
wolde on Godes þeowdome be his lárum lyfian.　He
þa se awyrgeda gast þæs ylcan preostes heortan and
geþanc mid his searwes attre geond sprengde[1] and
mengde; lærde hine se awyrgeda gast þæt he Guðlac
ofsloge and acwealde, and þus on his heortan ge-
sende: Gif ic hine ofslea and acwelle, þonne mæg
ic eft ágan þa ylcan stowe æfter him; and me þonne
woruld-men arwurðiað swa swa hi hine nu doð.
Ða gelamp hit sume dæge þæt se ylca preost com
to þam cadigan were þæt he hine wolde scyran, swá
his gewuna wæs ymbe twentig nihta, þæt he hine
wolde þwean, þa wæs he swyðe oflysted þæt he þæs
eadigan weres blod agute.　He þa sona Guðlac
gesceah þa láre þæs awyrgedan gastes, (swa him ealle
þa toweardan þing þurh Godes gifu wæron gecydde,

---

[1] MS. spregde.

him the weapon of the accursed spirits, and sang the psalm: Exurgat Ðeus et dissipentur, et reliqua. As soon as he had sung the first verse of the psalm, they departed like smoke from his presence. When the blessed man Guthlac thus frequently fought and contended against the cursed spirits, they perceived that their power and work was overcome.

VII.

Concerning Becccl the priest.

There was a priest whose name was Beccel; he came to the holy man and begged him that he would take him to him, and he promised that he would humbly live in God's service by his instructions. Then the accursed spirit sprinkled and watered over with the poison of his deceit the heart and mind of this same priest; the cursed spirit advised him that he should smite and kill Guthlac; and thus suggested to his heart: If I slay and kill him, then may I afterwards possess this same place after him; and men of the world will then honour me as they now do him. It happened one day that the same priest came to the holy man to shave him (as his custom was every twenty days to wash himself); then was he vehemently tempted to shed the blood of the blessed man. Guthlac soon perceived the persuasion of the cursed spirit (as all future things were through

and eac swylce þa andweardan, and he mihte þone
man innan geseon and geondsceawian swá útan,)
and he cwæð þus to him : Eala þu min Beccel to
hwan hafast _{þu} bedigled under þam dysigan breoste
þone awyrgedan feond? for hwon nelt _{þu} þæs biteran
attres þa deaþ-berendan wæter of þe aspiwan? ic þæt
geseo þæt þu eart fram þam awyrgedan gaste beswicen,
and þa mánfullan smeaunge þiure heortan ; manna-
kynnes costere and middaneardes feond hafað
acenned on þe þa unablinnu þæs yfelan geþohtes ; ac
ahwyrf þe fram þære yfelan láre þæs awyrgedan
gastes.   Ða ongeat he sona þæt he wæs fram þan
awyrgedan gaste beswícen ; feol sona to þæs halgan
weres fotum, and þa sona mid tearum him his synne
andette.   He þa sona se halga wer Guðlac, na læs
þæt án þæt he him þa synne forgeaf, ac eac swylce
he him gehet þæt he him wolde beon on fultume on
eallum his earfeþum.

VIII.

Hu þa deofla ferdon.

Ðæt gelamp sumere nihte þa se halga wer
Guðlac his gebedum befeal, þa gehyrde he gry-
metunga[1] hryþera and mislicra wildeora.   Næs
þa nan hwil to þam þæt he geseah ealra wihta
and wildeora and wurma hiw in cuman to him.
Ærest he geseah leon ansyne, and he mid his

---

[1] MS. grymetigenda.

God's grace known to him, and also present things, and he could see and look through the man within as well as without) ; and he said thus to him : Oh ! my Beccel, wherefore hast thou concealed under thy foolish breast the accursed fiend? why wilt thou not spit out from thee the death-bearing waters of that bitter poison? I perceive that thou art deceived by the accursed spirit, and I see the wicked device of thy heart. The tempter of mankind and the enemy of earth hath begotten in thee the unrest of this evil intent; but turn thyself away from the evil teaching of the accursed spirit. Then perceived he that he had been deceived by the accursed spirit, fell at the holy man's feet, and with tears confessed to him his sin. Thereupon the holy man Guthlac not only forgave him the sin, but also promised him that he would be his helper in all his trials.

VIII.

How the devils departed.

It happened one night, when the holy man Guthlac fell to his prayers, he heard the howlings of cattle and various wild beasts. Not long after he saw the appearances of animals and wild beasts and creeping things coming in to him. First he saw the visage of a lion, that threatened him with his bloody tusks;

blódigum tuxum to him beotode; swylce eac fearres
gelicnysse, and beran ansyne, þonne hi gebolgene
beoð.   Swylce eac næddrena híw, and swynes gry-
metunge, and wulfa geþeot, and hræfena cræcetunge,[1]
and mislice fugela hwistlunge; þæt hi woldon mid
heora hiwunge þæs halgan weres mod awendan.
He þa se halga wer Guþlac hine gewæpnode mid
þan wæpue þære Cristes róde, and mid þam scylde
þæs halgan geleafan, and forseah þa costunge þara
awyrgedra gasta, and þus cwæð: Eala þu earma
wiðerwearda gast, þin mægn ys gesyne, and þin miht
ys gecyþed: þu nu earma, wildeora and fugela and
wyrma hiw ætywest,[2] þu iu þe ahofe þæt þu woldest
beon gelic þam ecan Gode.   Nu þonne ic bebeode
þe on þam naman þæs ecan Godes, se þe worhte
and þe of heofones heannysse awearp, þæt þu fram
þisse[3] ungeþwærnysse gestille.   þa sona æfter þon
calle þa ætywnysse þara awerigdra gasta onweg ge-
wáton.[4]

IX.
legiten
Hu þæt gewrit ~~begæn~~ wæs.

Ðæt gelamp on sumere nihte, þæt þær com sum
man to þæs halgan weres spræce. Mid þy he þær
dagas wunode, þa gelamp hit þæt he sum gewrit
awrat on cartan. þa he þa hæfde þæt gewrit

[1] MS. cræcetung.   [2] MS. ætywes.   [3] MS. þisum.   [4] MS. gewát.

also the likeness of a bull, and the visage of a bear, as when they are enraged. Also he perceived the appearance of vipers, and a hog's grunting, and the howling of wolves, and croaking of ravens, and the various whistling of birds; that they might, with their fantastic appearance, divert the mind of the holy man. Then the holy man Guthlac armed himself with the weapon of Christ's cross, and with the shield of holy faith, and despised the temptation of the accursed spirits, and spake thus: O! thou wretched rebellious spirit, thy power is seen and thy might is made known: thou, wretched one, now displayest the forms of wild beasts and birds and creeping things, thou who once exaltedst thyself that thou mightest be equal to the eternal God. Now then I command thee, in the name of the eternal God, who made thee, and cast thee down from the height of heaven, that thou cease from this troubling. Immediately thereafter all the appearances of the accursed spirits went away.

IX.

How the writing was recovered.

It happened one night that there came one to speak with the holy man. When he had remained some days there, it fell out that he wrote some writing on a sheet of paper. When he had written

awriten, þa eode he ut. Ða com þær sum hrefen
inn ; sona swá he þa cartan geseah þa genam he hig
sona and gewat mid on þæne fenn. Sona swa se
foresǽda cuma ongean com, þa geseah he þone
hrefen þa cartan beran þa wæs he sona swyðe
unbliþe. Ða wæs on þam ylcan timan þæt se̩ halga
wer Gutðlac ut of his cyrcan eode ; þa geseah he
þone broþor sarig. þa frefrode he hine and him to
cwæð : Ne beo þu broþor sarig ; ac swa se hrefen
þurh þa fennas upp afligeð, swá þu him æfter row ;
þonne metest þu þæt gewrit. Næs þa nænig hwil
to þan þæt he to scipe eode se ylca þe þæt gewrit
wrat. Mid þy he þurh þa fenland reow, þa com he
to sumum mere þe wel neah þæt egland wæs : þa
wæs þær on middan þam mere sum hreod-bed ; þa
hangode seo carte on þam hreode efne swa hig
mannes hand þær ahengce : and he sona þa bliþe
feng to þære cártan, and he wundriende to þam
Godes were brohte : and he þa se eadiga wer Guthlac
sǽde þæt þæt nǽre his geearnung ac Godes mild-
heortnys.[1] Wæron on þam ylcan yglande twegen
hrefnas gewunode, to þæs gifre, þæt swa hwæt swa
hi mihton gegripan þæt hi þæt woldon onweg
alǽdan ; and he þeah hwæþere heora gifernysse
ealle æbær and geþolode, þæt he eft sealde mannum
bysene his geþyldes ; and na læs þæt an þæt him þa
fugelas underþeodde wǽron, ac eac swa þa fixas, and
wilde deor þæs westenes ealle hi him hyrdon, and

---

[1] MS. mildheortnysse.

the writing he went out. There came a raven in; as soon as he saw the paper he took it and went with it to the fen. As soon as the aforesaid guest came back again, he saw the raven carrying the paper; thereat was he very vexed. It happened at that time that the holy man Guthlac came out of his church; there saw he the brother grieving. He consoled him, and said: Be not grieved, brother; but when the raven flies up through the fens row thou after him; so shalt thou recover the writing. Not long after he went into a boat, the same man namely who had written the writing. Having rowed through the fenlands, he came to a mere, which was very near the island; there was in the midst of the mere a bed of reeds; there hung the paper on the reeds, even as though man's hand had hanged it there; and he forthwith joyfully seized the paper, and brought it wondering to the man of God. And the blessed man Guthlac said that it was not the effect of his merit, but of God's mercy. There were settled on the same island two ravens, so greedy that whatsoever they could seize they would carry away; and notwithstanding he bore and endured all their greediness, that he might give men the example of his patience. And not only were the birds subject to him, but also the fishes and wild beasts of the wilderness all obeyed him, and he daily

hc hym dæghwamlice andlyfene sealde of his agenre[1]
handa, swa heora gecynde wæs.

X.

Hu þa swalawan on him sǽton and sungon.

þæt gelamp sume siþe þæt þær com sum arwurþe
broðor to him, þæs nama wæs Wilfrið, se him wæs
geara on gastlicum[2] þoftscipe geþeoded. Mid þan
þe hig þa on manegum gespræcum heora gastlic lif
smeadon, þa comon þær sæmninga in twa swalewan
fleogan, and hi efne blissiende heora sang úpahofon,
and þa æfter þon hi setton unforhtlice on þa sculdra
þæs halgan weres Guðlaces, and hi þær heora sang
upahofon; and hi eft setton on his breost and on his
earmas and on his cneowu. Ða hi þa Wilfrið lange
þa fugelas wundriende beheold, þa frægn hine
Wilfriþ forhwon þa wildan fugelas þæs widgillan
westenes swa eadmodlice him on sǽton. He þa se
halga wer Guðlac him andswarode and him to cwæð:
Ne leornodest þu broðor Wilfrið on halgum gewritum,
þæt se þe on Godes willan his lif leofode, þæt hine
wilde deor and wilde fugelas þe near wǽron; and
se man þe hine wolde fram woruld-mannum his lif
libban, þæt hine englas þe néar comon: forþon se
þe woruldlicra manna spræce gelomlice wilnað, þonne
ne mæg he þa engellican spræce befeolan.

[1] MS. agenra.   [2] MS. gastlicre.

gave them food from his own hand, as suited their kind.

X.

How the swallows sat upon him and sung.

It happened on a time that there came a venerable brother to him whose name was Wilfrith, who had of old been united with him in spiritual fellowship. Whilst they discussed in many discourses their spiritual life, there came suddenly two swallows flying in, and behold they raised up their song rejoicing; and after that they sat fearlessly on the shoulders of the holy man Guthlac, and then lifted up their song; and afterwards they sat on his bosom and on his arms and his knees. When Wilfrith had long wondering beheld the birds, he asked him wherefore the wild birds of the wide waste so submissively sat upon him. The holy man Guthlac answered him and said: Hast thou never learnt, brother Wilfrith, in holy writ, that he who hath led his life after God's will, the wild beasts and wild birds have become the more intimate with him. And the man who would pass his life apart from worldly men, to him the angels approach nearer. But he who frequently longeth for the converse of worldly men cannot meet with angelic discourse.

XI.

Ymb þa glofan þe þa hrefnas bæron.

Swylce eac gelamp sume siþe witedomlic[1] wundor be þisum halgan were. Wæs sum fore-mæra man æþelan kyne-kynnes on Myrcna-ríce, þæs nama wæs Æþelbald. þa wolde he to þæs halgan weres spræce cuman : beget þa æt Wilfriðe þæt he hine to þam Godes were gelædde ; and hi þa sona on scipe eodon, and ferdon to þam yglande þær se halga wer Guthlac on wæs. Ða hi þa to þam halgan were comon, þa hæfde Wilfrið forlæten his glofan on þam scipe : and hi þa wið þone halgan wer spræcon, he þa se eadiga wer Guthlac acsode hi hwæðer hi ænig þingc[2] æfter heom on þam scipe forleton, (swa him God ealle þa diglan þingc cuð gedyde) : þa andswarode him Wilfrið and cwæð þæt he forlete his twa glofan on þam scipe. Næs þa nænig hwil to þan sona swa hi ut of þam inne[3] eodon, þa gesegon hi þone hræfn mid þan sweartan nebbe þa glofe teran uppe on anes huses þæce. He þa sona se halga wer Guðlac þone hrefn mid his worde þreade for his reþnysse, and he þa his worde[4] hyrsumode, swa fleah se fugel west ofer þæt westen ; he þa Wilfrið mid gyrde of þæs[5] huses hrofe þa glofe geræhte. Swylce næs eac nænig hwil to þam sona comon þær þry men to þære hyðe, and þær tacn slogon. þa sona

---

[1] MS. witedomlice.   [2] MS. þinc.   [3] MS. in.
[4] MS. worda.   [5] MS. þam.

XI.

Concerning the gloves which the ravens carried off.

Also there happened on a time a prophetic miracle by this holy man. There was a distinguished man of noble king's-kindred in Mercia, whose name was Athelbald. He wished to come to converse with the holy man. He prevailed upon Wilfrith that he should bring him to the man of God; and they went into a boat, and journeyed to the island whereon the holy man Guthlac was. When they had come to the holy man, behold Wilfrith had left his glove in the boat. And while they conversed with the holy man, he, the blessed man Guthlac, asked them whether they had left anything behind them in the boat (for God made known to him all secret things); then answered Wilfrith, and said that he had left his two gloves in the boat. Not long after, as soon as they had gone out of the house, there they saw the raven with his black beak tearing the glove upon the roof of a house. Then the holy man Guthlac rebuked with his word the raven for his mischief, and it obeyed his word, and the bird flew westward over the wilderness; whereupon Wilfrith reached the glove from the roof of the house with a stick. Also not long after there came three men to the landing-place, and there sounded the signal.

eode se halga wer Guðlac út to þam mannum mid
bliðum andwlite and góde mode; he þa spæc wið
þam mannum.   Mid þan þe hi faran woldon, þa
brohton hi forð ane glofe, sædon þæt heo of anes
hrefnes muþe feolle.   He se halga wer Guþlac sona
to-smerciende feng, and heom his bletsunge sealde,
and hi eft ferdon; and he eft ageaf þa glofe þam þe
hi ær ahte.

XII.

Hu Hwætred his bælo[1] onfeng.

Wæs on East-Engla-lande sum man æþeles cynnes
þæs nama wæs Hwætred.   Mid þy he þa dæghwamlice mid arfæstnysse his ealderum underþeoded wæs,
hit gelamp sume siðe þa he æt his fæder hame wæs,
þæt hine se awyrgeda gast him oneode þæt he of
his gewitte wearð, and hine se awyrgeda feond swa
swyþe swencte mid þære wodnysse þæt he hys
agenne lichaman[2] mid irene ge eac mid his tópum
blodgode and wundode; and na læs þæt an þæt he
hine sylfne swa mid þam wælhreowum tópum
wundode ac eac swa hwylcne swá he mihte þæt he
swá gelíce tær.   Ða gelamp sume siþe þæt þær wæs
mycel menigo manna gegaderod his maga and eac
oþra his neh-freonda, þæt hi hine woldon gebindan
and don hine gewyldne: he þa genam sum twibil,
and mid þan þry men to deaðe ofsloh, and oþre

---

[1] MS. hæla.   [2] MS. agene lichama.

Then went the holy man Guthlac out to the men
with cheerful countenance and good humour, and
there spoke with them.   When they wished to depart they brought forth a glove, and said that it had
fallen from a raven's mouth.   The holy man Guthlac
received it smiling, and gave them his blessing,
and they then departed; and afterwards he gave
the glove to him who before owned it.

XII.

How Hwætred received his health.

There was in the land of the East-Angles a man
of noble kin, whose name was Hwætred.   Whereas
he was daily reverently subject to his elders, it
happened on a time, while he was at his father's
house, that the accursed spirit entered into him, so
that he went out of his wits, and the accursed spirit
afflicted him so severely with this madness, that he
bloodied and wounded his own body as well with
iron as with his teeth; and not himself only did he
wound with his ferocious teeth, but also whomsoever
he could he in like manner tore.   It happened on
a time that there was a great multitude of men
gathered together of his kinsmen, and also of other
his near friends, that they might bind him and bring
him into subjection.   Thereupon he took an axe,
and with it smote three men to death, and wounded

manige mid gesarode.   Þæs þa feowor gear þæt he
swá wæs mid þære wodnysse swiðe geswenced.   Þa
wæs he æt nextan genumen fram his magum, and to
halgum mynstre gelæd, to þon þæt hine mæsse-
preostas and bisceopas wið þa wodnysse þwean and
clænsian sceoldon.   And hi hwæþere on menigum
þingum ne mihton þa yfelan mægn þæs awyrgdan
gastes ofadrifan.   Ða æt nextan hi eft ham únrote
mid þam mæge ferdon, and hi him deaþes swyðor
uþon þonne he lengc þa men drehte, ða wæs æt
nextan gemærsod se hlisa on þone[1] þeodscipe þæt on
þam fenne-middum on anum eglande þe Cruwland
hatte wære sum ancra þe[2] missenlicum mægnum
for Gode weohse.   Hi þa sona, þa hi þær þone
halgan wer acsodon, þohton þæt hi woldon þær þone
man gebringan, gif þæt Godes stihtung wǽre
þæt hi þær áre findan mihton.   And hi hit swa
gefremedon, ferdon þyder þæt hi comon to sumum
yglande þe wel neah wæs þam eglande þe se Godes
man on wæs; and þær wǽron on niht mid þan
seocan men.   Þa hit þa on mergen dæg wæs, þa
comon hi to þam[3] foresprecenan eglande, and þa
mid þan gewunelican þeawe tacen slogon.   He þa
sona se halga wer Guðlac to heom eode mid healice
mægne Godes lufan: þa hi þa heora intingan him
wepende sǽdon, þa wæs he sona mid mildheortnysse
gefylled.   Genam þa sona þone untruman man and
hine lædde into his cyrican, and þær þry dagas

---

[1] MS. ꝥ.   [2] MS. ꝥ.   [3] MS. þære.

many others with them. It was four years that he
was sorely afflicted with this madness. Then was he
at last taken by his relations and brought to the holy
monastery, to the end that mass-priests and bishops
might wash and cleanse him from his madness.
And they, however, with many expedients, could
not drive out the evil powers of the accursed spirit.
When at last they went home sorrowful with their
relative, and they rather wished him dead than that
he should longer annoy men, then at length the report
was spread in the province that in the midst of the
fen, on an island which was called Crowland, was
an anchorite, who flourished before God with various
virtues. Then they forthwith, when they heard of
the holy man, thought that they would take the
man thither, if it were God's providence that they
might there find help. And they performed this,
journeyed thither till they came to an island, which
was very near that on which the man of God was,
and they were there during the night with the sick
man. When it was day on the morrow, they came
to the aforesaid island; then in the usual manner
sounded a signal. Then forthwith the holy man
Guthlac went to them in the fervent power of God's
love. When they weeping had told him their affair,
he was filled with pity. He took the sick man and
led him into his church, and there remained three

singallice on his gebedum áwunode. Þa on þam
þriddan dæge þa sunne upeode, þa baþode he hine
on gehalgedum wætre, and bleow on his ansyne and
mid þan eall þæt mægn þæs awyrgedan gastes on
him gebræc: and he þa se ylca man swa he of
hefegum slæpe raxende awoce, and he eft to his
hælo feng, and ham ferde; and him næfre syþþan
þa hwile þe he leofode seo adl[1] ne eglode.

XIII.

Be Aþelbaldes gefere.

Swilce eac gelamp on sumne sæl þæt þæs foresprecenan wræccan Aþelbaldes gefere þæs nama
wæs Ecga þæt he wæs fram þam awyrgedan gaste
unstille; and swá swyþe he hine drehte þæt he his
sylfes nænig gemynd ne hæfde. Hi þa his magas
hine to þam Godes men gelæddon. Ða sona þæs
þe he to him com, þa begyrde he hine mid his
gyrðele. Næs þa nænig hwil to þan sona swa he
wæs mid þam gyrdele begyrd, eal seo unclænnys[2]
fram him gewát, and him syþþan næfre seo adl[3] ne
eglode. Eac se[4] eadiga wer Guðlac witedomlice
gaste weox and fremede, and he þa toweardan
mannum cydde swa cuðlice swa þa andweardan.

---

[1] MS. adle.   [2] MS. unclænnysse.   [3] MS. adle.   [4] MS. þone.

days incessantly at his prayers. When the sun rose on the third day, he bathed him in holy water and blew in his face, and with that all the power of the accursed spirit upon him was shattered : and this same man was as though he had awoke from a deep slumber, and he received his health again, and went home; and the illness never ailed him afterwards so long as he lived.

XIII.

Concerning Athelbald's follower.

Also it happened on a time that a follower of the aforesaid exile Athelbald, whose name was Ecga, was disquieted by the accursed spirit. And he plagued him so severely that he had no recollection of himself. Then his relations brought him to the man of God. As soon as he came to him he girded him with his girdle. No sooner was he girded with the girdle than all the uncleanness departed from him, and the illness never after ailed him. Also the blessed man Guthlac flourished and prospered in the prophetic spirit, and he made known future things to men, as clearly as the present things.

XIV.

Be þam abbode.

Þæt gelamp sume siþe þæt þær com sum abbod to
him þe him wæsgeara on gastlicum[1] þoftscipe geþeoded. Þa he þa þyder ferde þa wæron his hand-þegnas
twegen, bædon hyne þurh leofe-bene þæt hi moston
on oðerne weg faran, and sædon þæt him þæs neod
wǽre and eac þearf. Þa gcuþe him þæs se abbod
þæs þe hi hine bǽdon. Ða he þa se abbod þær com
to þære spræce þæs eadigan weres Guðlaces, mid þan
hi þa sylfe betweonum drencton[2] of þam willan
haligra gewrita, þa betwyx þa halgan gewritu þe hi
spræcon ða cwæð Guðlac to him: Ac hwyder
gewiton þa twegen þe ǽr fram þe cyrdon? Þa andswarode he him and cwæð: Hi bǽdon lǽfe[3] ǽt me
wæs heom oþer intinga[4] þæt hi hider cuman ne
mihton. He þa Guðlac him andswarode (swa him
God ealle þa toweardan þing onwreah, þæt him
wǽron swa cuðe swa þa andweardan), ongan him þa
secgan þone sið þara broþra and him cwæð to: Hi
ferdon þær to sumre wydewan ham and þær wæron
ondrencte mid oferdrynce. And na læs þæt an þæt
he him þone heora siþ sǽde, ac eac swilce be heora
andleofone, ge eac swilce þa sylfan word þe hi þær
spræcon, eall he be endebyrdnysse him gerehte.
Mid þan þe se abbod his bletsunge hæfde onfangen,
he þa eft ferde. Mid þy þe þa foresprecenan broþra

[1] MS. gastlicre.   [2] MS. dremdon.   [3] MS. læfa.   [4] MS. intingan.

XIV.

Concerning the abbot.

It happened on a time that there came an abbot to him, who was formerly united with him in spiritual communion. While he journeyed thither his two attendants were with him; they supplicated him with a request for leave that they might go another way, and said that there was need and necessity for them to do this. Then the abbot granted them that which they begged of him. When the abbot came there to conversation with the blessed man Guthlac, whilst they mutually gave each other to drink from the well of the sacred scriptures, then amidst their talk of the sacred scriptures Guthlac said to him: But whither went the two that erewhile turned back from thee? Then answered he him, and said: They begged leave of me; they had another affair, so that they could not come hither. Then Guthlac answered him, (as God revealed to him all future things, which were as well known to him as the present,) and began to tell him the way of these brothers, and said to him: They went to the house of a widow, and were there intoxicated with too much drinking. And not only did he tell him of their road, but also concerning their fare, as also the very words which they there spake; he related it all to him in order. When the abbot had received his blessing he departed. When the afore-

eft to þam abbode comon, þa fregn he hi hwær hi
wæron.   þa andswarodon hi him and cwædon þæt hi
wæron on heora nyd-þearfum swyðe geswencte.   þa
axode he hi hwæþer hit swá wære; þa swóron hi
swiðe þæt hit swa wǽre.   þa cwæð he to him : Ac
to hwon sweriað git mán; ac wæron æt þisse
wydewan hame and þær þus yucer lif leofodon and
þisum wordum þus þær spræcon? þa ongeaton hi
heora misdæda, feollon þa to his fotum and him
forgifenysse bædon, and him andetton þæt hit wære
swa he ǽr sæde.

XV.

Be þam broþrum þe him to comon.

Comon eac swylce twegen broðra to him on
sumne sæl of sumum mynstre. þa hi þa þyder-
weard ferdon, þa hæfdon hi mid heom twa flaxan
mid ælað gefylde ; þa gewearð him betweonan þæt
hi þa gehyddon under anre tyrf, þæt hi, þonne hi
ham ferdon, hæfdon eft mid him.   Ða hi þa to him
comon, þa trymede he hi mid his láre and mid his
manunge heora heortan intimbrede.   Mid þan þe
hi manig þing heom betweonum spræcon, ða se
eadiga wer Guðlac mid bliþum andwlitan and
hlihhendre[1] gespræce he cwæþ to heom : For hwon
behydde git þa flaxan under ane tyrf, and for hwon
ne læddon ge hi mid inc? Hi þa swyðe wundrodon

----

[1] MS. hlihhende.

said brothers again came to the abbot, he asked them where they had been. They answered him, and said that they had toiled much in their needful affairs. Then he asked them whether it were so. Then they swore stoutly that it was so. Then said he to them : Nay, but wherefore swear ye to a wicked lie ; for ye were at the house of such a widow, and there passed your time in such wise, and spake there such words! Then they were conscious of their misdeeds, fell at his feet, and begged forgiveness of him, and confessed that it was as he said.

XV.

Concerning the brothers who came to him.

Then came also to him two brothers on a time from a certain monastery. Whilst they journeyed thitherward they had with them two bottles filled with ale; then it was agreed between them that they should hide them under a turf, that, when they went home, they might have them with them. When they were come to him, he strengthened them with his counsel, and edified their hearts with his admonition. When they had spoken on many subjects amongst them, the blessed man Guthlac, with merry countenance and laughing words, said to them : Wherefore hid ye the bottles under a turf, and why brought ye them not with you ?

þara worda þæs halgan weres, and to him luton
and hine bletsunge bǽdon.   And he hi gebletsode,
and hi þa eft ham ferdon.   Wæs on þa sylfan tid
þæt þone foresprecenan wer missenlices hades men
sohton, ægðer þara ge ealdormen ge bisceopas, and
abbodas, and ælces hades heane and rice.   And na
læs þæt an þæt hine men sohton of þære heh-þeode
Mercna-rice, ac eac swylce ealle þa þe on Bretone
wǽron þe þisne cadigan wer hyrdon, þæt hi
æghwonon to him efston and scyndon; and þa þe
wǽron aþer oþþe on lichaman untrumnysse, oððe
fram þam awyrgdan gaste geswencte and numene,
oþþe oþrum yfelum, þe manna-cynn[1] mid missenlicum
sorgum and sarum útan ymbseald ys; and on heora
nænigum[2] se hiht awácode þe hi to him genamon;
forþan næs nænig untrum þæt he ungelacnod fram
him ferde; nænig deofol-seoc þæt he eft wel ge-
witfæst ne wǽre; ne on nænigre untrumnysse þæt
he ·eft gehǽled him fram ne ferde.

XVI.

Be Aþelbaldes gefere.

Ðæt gelamp mid þan þæt manigo men for missenlicum þingum him to comon, þa betweox oþre
com þær þæs foresprecenan wræccan Æþelbaldes
gefera þæs nama wæs Ova, þæt he wolde þone halgan
geneosian and wiþgesprecan.   Ða gelamp hit þan

---

[1] MS. manna-cynnes.   [2] MS. menigum.

They were greatly amazed at these words of the holy man, and bowed to him, and begged his blessing. And he blessed them, and they returned home. (It came to pass at that same time, that men of divers conditions sought the holy man, as well nobles as bishops and abbots, and men of every condition, poor and rich. And not only men sought him from the province of Mercia, but also all who in Britain heard of this holy man, hied and hastened to him from all quarters : and those who were either in sickness of body, or plagued and possessed by the cursed spirit, or other evils, as mankind is compassed about with various griefs and pains : and of none of those whom they brought to him were the hopes thwarted; for there was no sick person that went from him unhealed; no possessed person that did not come to his right wits again ; none afflicted with any disease that did not leave him cured.

XVI.

Concerning Athelbald's companion.

It came to pass when many men came to him for divers matters, among others came thither a companion of the before-mentioned exile Athelbald, whose name was Ova, that he might visit and converse with the saint. It happened on the second

æfteran dæge þæs þe he þyder on þære fóre wæs, þa
eode he ofer sumne þórn on niht; þa besloh se þorn
on þone fot, and swa strang wæs se sting þæs þornes
þæt he eode þurh þone fot, and he þa uneaðe þone
sið geferde, and þurh mycel gewinn he to þam foresprecenan eglande becom, þær se eadiga wer Guðlac
on eardode.   And mid þan þe he þær on niht wæs,
þa asweoll him se lichama ofer healf fram þam
lendenum _{oþþ}a fet, and swa sarlice he wæs mid þam
sare geswenced, þæt he naðer þara ne gesittan ne
standan mihte.   Mid _{þy} man[1] þæt þam Godes were
sæde Guðlace, þa bebead he þæt hine man to him
gelædde.   Þa he þa wæs broht to him, þa sæde he
to him þone intingan þurh hwæt he ærest swa
geþræst wǽre, and hu him ærest þæt earfoð on
becóme.   He þa sona Guðlac hine sylfne úngyrede,
and þæt reaf þe he genehlice on him hæfde he hine
slefde on þone foresprecenan man. Næs þa nænig
hwil to þon sona swa he mid þan hrægle swa miccles
weres gegyred wæs, þa ne mihte þæt þæt sar aberau.
He þa sona se ylca þórn, efne swá swá strǽl of
bogan astelleþ, swa he of þam man afleah, and on
þa fyrle gewát; and þa sona on þa sylfan tid eall se
swyle and eall þæt sár gewat fram him; and he
sona to þa sylfan tíd mid bliþum mode to þam
halgan were sprǽc and he eft þanon ferde butan
sceðnysse æniges sáres.   Swylce eac gelamp þæt
ealle þa men wundrodon þe þas þing gehyrdon, and
hi on þan wuldredon and heredon heofones God.

---

[1] MS. he.

day that he was on the journey thither, that he walked over a thorn in the night: the thorn stuck into his foot, and so strong was the prickle of the thorn that it went through the foot, and he with difficulty proceeded on his way, and with much effort he arrived at the fore-mentioned island, whereon the blessed man Guthlac dwelt. And when he was there at night, his body swelled, above half of it from the loins to the feet, and he was so grievously afflicted with the pain, that he could neither sit nor stand. As soon as they told this to Guthlac, the man of God, he ordered that he should be brought to him: when he was brought to him, he told him the cause through which he was first so tormented, and how that pain first came upon him. Thereupon Guthlac immediately stripped himself, and the garment which he wore next his skin he put upon the foresaid man. No sooner was he attired in the garment of so great a man, but the wound could not abide it: and lo! this same thorn, as an arrow speeds from the bow, so did it fly from the man, and go to a distance; and immediately at the same time all the swelling and all the wound departed from him, and he presently conversed with the holy man with blithe mood, and he afterwards went from thence without harm of any wound. And it came to pass that all men who heard these things wondered, and glorified and praised the God of heaven for them.

XVII.

Be þam halgan biscope Sce Hædde.

Swylce nys eac mid idele to forlætenne þæt
wundor þæt þurh witedomes cræft [he]¹ wiste and
cydde : forþon him wæs þurh Godes gife seald, þæt
he þa word þara æfwearda swa geara wiste swa þara
andwearda þe him foran gesæde wǽron.   Gelamp
sume siþe þæt sum bisceop to him ferde þæs nama
wæs Hædda, efne swa swa he wære mid heofonlicre
þeahte gelǽred þæt he to þære spræce ferde þæs
Godes mannes.   Þa hæfde se bisceop mid hine on
his geferscipe sumne man gelæredne, þæs nama wæs
Wigfrið.   Mid þan he þa betweox þa oðre þæs
bisceopes þegnas þyder ferde,² þa ongunnon hi fela
þinga be þam halgan were sprecan and fela þinga
be his wundrum sǽdon.   Sume hi þonne sǽdon þa
heardlicnysse his lifes, þa wundor þe he worhte ;
sume hi þonne twiendlice be his life sprǽcon, and
þæt cwǽdon þæt hi nyston hwæðer he on Godes
mihte þa þing worhte, þe þurh deofles cræft.   Þa
þa hi þas þing þus heom betweonon sprǽcon, þa
cwæþ se witega to heom : Ic mæg, cwæð he, cunnian
and gewitan hwæþer he biþ bigengca þære godcundan
æfæstnysse ; forþon ic wæs lange betwux Sceotta-
folc eardiende ; and ic geseah þær manige gode, and
on Godes þeodscipe wel heora lif læddon ; and hi
manigum wundrum and tacnum þurh Godes mihte

---

¹ MS. cræft wiste and him cydde.   ² MS. ferdon.

XVII.

Concerning the holy bishop St. Hædde.

Also we must not pass over with neglect that wondrous thing, how that with prophetic power he knew and made things known. For through God's grace it was given him, that he should know the words of the absent as easily as those of the present which were uttered before him. It happened on a time that a bishop came to him, whose name was Hædda, as though he were counselled by a heavenly thought, that he should go to speak with the man of God. The bishop had with him in his company a learned man, whose name was Wigfrith. Whilst he journeyed thither among the other attendants of the bishop, they began to say many things about the holy man, and spoke much of his miracles. Some of them then spake of the severity of his life, the miracles which he wrought; some then spake doubtingly of his life, and said that they knew not whether he wrought these things in the strength of God, or through craft of the devil. While they spake these things among themselves, the philosopher said to them: I am able, said he, to try and find out whether he be a cultivator of divine piety; for I was long dwelling among the Scotch people, and I saw there many good men, who led their life well in God's service; and they shone through God's power before the eyes of men, with many miracles

beforan manna eagum scinon. Of þara manna life
þe ic þær geseah ic mæg ongitan hu gerád þises
mannes lif ys, hwæþer he þurh Godes miht þa
wundor wyrceð, þe he þurh deofles miht deð. Mid
þy þa se[1] foresprecena bisceop to þære spræce becom
þæs Godes[2] mannes Guðlaces, hi þa sylfe betweonum
indrencton mid þam cerenum þære godspellican
swetnysse. Wæs on þam eadigan were Guðlace seo
beorhtnys þære Drihtnes gife swa swyþe scinende,
þæt swa hwæt swa he bodode and lærde, swa he of
engcellicre spræce þa word bodode and ræde. Wæs
eac swiðe mycel wisdóm on him, heofonlice snyttro,
þæt swa hwæt swa he gelærde þæt he þæt trymede
mid þa godcundan [bysena][3] haligra gewrita. And
he þa semninga se bisceop, on midre þære spræce
þe hi heom betwux smeadon, eadmodlice to þam
Godes were geleat and hine geornlice bæd and
halsode þæt he þurh hine sacerdlice þenunge onfengce,
þæt he hine moste gehádigan to mæsse-preoste and
to þenunge Drihtnes weofodes. He þa sona Guðlac
his benum[4] geþafode, and he hine sylfne to eorðan
astrehte, and þæt cwæð þæt he wolde þæs þe Godes
willa wære and þæs biscopes. þa hi þa hæfdon þa
þenunge gefylled and he wæs gehalgod, swá ic ær
sæde, he þa se biscop bæd þone halgan wer þæt he
scolde to gercorde fón mid him : and he þa swa
dyde þeah hit his life ungeþeawe wære. þa hi þa to
gercorde sæton, swa ic ær sæde, þa locode Guthlac

---

[1] MS. þe.   [2] MS. gódes.   [3] [bysena] not in MS.   [4] MS. benun.

the bishop's attendants; then he saw the aforesaid brother Wigfrith, and spake thus to him: And now, brother Wigfrith, what sort of man seemeth thee now the priest is of whom thou saidst yesterday that thou wouldst try whether he were good or bad? Then Wigfrith arose, and bowed to the earth, and confessed his fault to him. Then the holy man was forthwith reconciled to him, and gave and granted him his pardon. The hallowing of the island of Crowland, and also of the blessed man Guthlac, took place at harvest-time, five days before St. Bartholomew's mass.

XVIII.

Concerning abbess Ecgburh.

It happened also on a time that the venerable maid Ecgburh, abbess, the daughter of Aldwulf the king, sent to the venerable man Guthlac a leaden coffin, and winding-sheet thereto, and besought him by the holy name of the celestial King, that after his departure they should place his body therein. She sent the message by a brother of worthy life, and bid him ask him, who should be the keeper of the place after him. When he had kindly received the message of the venerable maid, then concerning that which he was asked—who should be the

stówe hyrde æfter him bcon scolde, þa andswarode
he and cwæð, þæt se man wære on hǽþenum folce,
and þa git nǽre gefullod; ac þeah hwæþere þæt he
þa sona come[1] and þa gerynu sceolde onfon fulluht-
bæþes.   And hit eac swá gelamp: forþon se ylca
Cissa, se þe eft þa stowe heold, he com þæs ymb
litel fæc on Bretone and hine man þær gefullode,
swá se Godes wer foresǽde.

XIX.

Be Aðelbalde þam kyninge.

Swylce nys eac mid idelnysse to forelætenne þæt
wundor þe þes halga wer Guthlac foresǽde and
mannum cydde.   Wæs on sumre tide þæt com se
foresprecena wrǽcca to him Aþelbald; and hine
Ceolred se kyning hider and þider wide aflymde,
and he his ehtnysse and his hatunge fleah and
scúnode.   Ða com he to þære spæce þæs halgan
weres Guðlaces; þaþa se mennisca[2] fultum him
beswác, hine þeah hwæþere se godcunda fultum
gefrefrode.   Mid þy he þa to þam Godes were com,
and he him his earfoða rehto, þa cwæð Guðlac þus
to him: Eala min cniht þinra gewinna and earfoða
ic com únforgitende; ic forþon þe gemiltsode, and
for þinum earfoðum ic bæd God þæt he þe gemiltsode and þe gefultomode; and he þa mine béne
gehyrde, and he þe syleþ rice and anweald þinre

<hr>

[1] MS. com.   [2] MS. mennisce.

keeper of the place after him,—he answered and said, that the man was of heathen race, and was not yet baptised; but notwithstanding, that he should soon come, and should receive the rites of baptism. And so it came to pass; for the same Cissa, who afterwards held the place, came to Britain a little time afterwards, and they baptised him there, as the man of God foretold.

XIX.

Concerning Athelbald the king.

Also we must not pass over with neglect the wonder which this holy man Guthlac foretold and made known to men. It happened on a time that the before-mentioned exile Athelbald came to him; and Ceolred the king hunted him hither and thither, far and wide, and he fled from and shunned his persecutions and his malice. He had recourse then to the conversation of the holy man Guthlac; for when human help had failed him, notwithstanding divine support comforted him. When he came to the man of God, and related to him his troubles, Guthlac spake thus to him : O ! my son, I am not forgetful of thy conflicts and thy troubles; for this cause I took pity on thee, and for thy troubles I prayed God that he would have pity on thee, and support thee; and he has heard my prayer, and he will give thee kingdom and rule over thy people,

þeode, and þa ealle fleoð beforan þe þa þe hatiað, and þin sweord fornymeð ealle þine þa wiþerweardan, forþon Drihten þe bið on fultume. Ac be þu geþyldig, forþon ne begitest þu na þæt rice on gerisne woruldlicra þinga, ac mid Drihtnes fultume þu þin rice begytest; forþon Drihten þa genyþerað þe þe nu hatiað, and Drihten afyrreð þæt rice fram him and hæfð þe gemynt and geteohhod. Þa he þas word gehyrde, he þa sona Aþelbald his hiht and his geleafan on God sylfne trymede, and he getrywode and gelyfde ealle þa þing þe se halga wer foresæde, þæt ricu[1] beoð onwende and ofánumene and hit á to þam ende efesteð ; and se ríca and se heana, se gelæreda and se ungelærda, and geong and eald, ealle hi gelice se stranga deað forgripeð and nymð.

XX.

Be þæs halgan weres lifes lenge and be his forðfore.

Ða gelámp hit on fyrste æfter þissum þæt se leofa Godes þeow Guthlac æfter þon fiftyne gear þe he Gode willigende lædde his lif, þa wolde God his þonc leofan þeow of þam gewinne þisse worulde yrmþa gelædan to þære ecan reste þæs heofoncundan rices. Ða gelamp on sumuc sæl mid þy he on his cyrcan æt his gebedum wæs, þa wæs he semninga mid adle gestanden. And he sona ongeat þæt him

[1] MS. rice.

and they shall flee before thee who hate thee; and thy sword shall destroy all thy adversaries, for the Lord is thy support. But be thou patient, for thou shalt not get the kingdom by means of worldly things, but with the Lord's help thou shalt get thy kingdom. For the Lord shall bring down those who now hate thee, and the Lord shall remove the kingdom from them, and hath remembered and appointed thee. When he heard these words, Athelbald soon fixed his hope and faith on God himself, and he trusted and believed all the things which the holy man foretold,—how that kingdoms are overturned and taken away, and are evermore hastening to an end; and the rich and the poor, the learned and the unlearned, and young and old,—all these alike, strong death clutcheth and taketh.

XX.

Concerning the length of the holy man's life, and his departure.

It happened, some while after this, that God's beloved servant Guthlac, after that he had led a life serving God for fifteen years,—then God pleased to lead his dear servant from the conflict of this world's miseries to the eternal rest of the heavenly kingdom. It happened on a time, when he was in his church at his prayers, he was suddenly attacked with illness. And he soon perceived that God's hand was sent

wæs Godes hand to sended, and he swyþe gebliþe
hine het gyrwan to þam ingange þæs heofonlican
rices.　Wæs he seofon dagas mid þære adle geswenced, and þæs eahtoþan dæges[1] he wæs to þam
ytemestan gelǽded.　þa gestod hine seo[2] adl þon
wodnesdæge[3] nebst eastron and þa eft þan ylcan
dæge on þære eastor-wucan he þæt lif of þam
lichaman sende.　Wæs sum broðor mid him þæs
nama wæs Beccel, þurh þone ic þa forðfore ongeat
þæs cadigan weres.　Mid þy he þa com þy dæge þe
hine seo adl[4] gestod, þa acsode he hine be ge-
hwilcum þingum.　þa andswarode he him lætlice,
and mid langre sworetunge þæt orð of þam breostum
teah.　þa he þa geseah þone halgan wer swá ún-
rotes modes, þa cwæð he to him : Hwæt gelamp
þe nywes nu ða ; ac þe on þysse nihte sum untrumnys[5] gelamp?　þa andswarode he him and him
cwæð to : Adl[6] me gelámp on þisse nihte.)　þa
frǽgn he eft hine : Wast þu min fǽder þone intingan
þiure adle oþþe to hwylcum ende wenest þu þæt seo
mettrumnys[7] wylle gelimpan?　þa andswarode he
him eft se halga wer and him cwæð to : Þeos[8] ongi-
tenys minre untrumnysse ys, þæt of þisum lichaman
sceal beon se gast alǽded ; forþon þan eahtoþan
dæge[9] bið ende þære minre mettrumnysse ; forþon
þæt gedafenað þæt se gast beo gegearwod, þæt ic

[1] MS. dæge.　　[2] MS. se.　　[3] MS. wodnes dæg.　　[4] MS. adle.
[5] MS. untrumnysse.　　[6] MS. adle.　　[7] MS. mettrumnysse.
[8] MS. þes ongitenysse.　　[9] MS. dæg.

upon him, and he right gladly began to prepare himself for his entry into the heavenly kingdom. He was seven days afflicted with the malady, and on the eighth day he was brought to the utmost extremity. The malady attacked him on the Wednesday next before Easter, and on the same day of the Easter-week after he gave forth his life from his body. (There was a brother with him whose name was Beccel, through whom I have been informed concerning the departure of the blessed man. When he came to him on the day when the sickness seized him, he asked him concerning certain things. And he answered him slowly, and drew the breath from his chest with long sighing. When he saw the holy man in so distressful mood, he said to him : What new thing has now happened to thee; has some sickness befallen thee on this night? Then he answered him and said to him : Sickness has befallen me this night.) Then again he asked him : Knowest thou, my father, the cause of thy sickness, or to what end thinkest thou that this illness will come? Then again the holy man answered and said to him : The meaning of my illness is this, that the spirit must be taken away from this body; for on the eighth day there will be an end of my illness; therefore it behoves that the spirit be prepared, that

mæg Gode filian.   Þa he þa þas word gehyrde se
foresprecena broðor Beccel, he þa swyþe weop and
geomrian ongan and mid mycelre uneðnysse his
eago-spind mid tearum gelomlice leohte.   Þa frefrode
hine se Godes wer Guthlac and him cwæð to : Min
bearn, ne beo þu na geúnrotsod forþon ne bið me
nǽnig úneþnys[1] þæt ic to Drihtne minum Gode
fare.   Wæs swa mycel rumnes on him þæs halgan
geleafan and swa mycele he to þære Godes lufan
hæfde, þæt se, cuþa and se uncuþa ealle him wæs
gelíce gesegen on gódum dǽdum.   Ða þæs ymbe
feower niht com se forma easter-dæg, he þa se eadiga
wer Guðlac on þære his mettrumnysse Gode lac
onsægde and mǽssan sáng, and syþþan he þa déor-
wyrþan lác offrode Cristes blodes, þa ongan he þam
foresprecenan breþer godspellian ; and he hine swa
swyþe deoplice mid his láre ineode, þæt he nǽfre ǽr
ne syþþan swylc ne gehyrde.   Mid þan þe [se][2]
seofoða dæg com þære his mettrumnysse, þa com se
foresprecena broðor on þære sixtan tide þæs dæges,
þæt he hine geneosian wolde : þa gemette he hine
hleonian on þam hale his cyrcan wið þam weofode.
Þa hwæþere he ne mihte wið hine sprecau, forþon
he geseah þæt his untrumnys[3] hine swyþe swencte :
þa þeah hwæþere he hine æfter þon bæd þæt he his
word to him forlete ǽr þon þe he swulte.   He þa
se eadiga wer Guþlac hwæt-hwego fram þam wage
þa werigan limu ahóf, cwæð þa þus to him : Min

---

[1] MS. uneþnysse.   [2] [se] not in MS.   [3] MS. untrumnysse.

I may go to God. When the aforesaid brother Beccel heard these words, he wept much and began to lament, and in great grief incessantly moistened his cheeks with tears. Then the man of God Guthlac comforted him, and said to him: My son, be not thou grieved, for to me it is no sorrow that I am going to the Lord my God. There was in him such a depth of holy faith, and so great love of God had he thereto, that the known and the unknown was entirely alike in his sight in respect of good deeds. When after four nights the first Easter-day arrived, the blessed man Guthlac in his sickness performed service to God, and sang mass, and after that he offered up the precious sacrifice of Christ's blood, he began to preach the gospel to the aforesaid brother; and he penetrated him so deeply with his counsel, that he never before nor after heard the like. When the seventh day of his illness came, then came the aforesaid brother at the sixth hour of the day to visit him. He found him leaning in the corner of his oratory, against the altar. Notwithstanding he might not speak to him, for he saw that his malady violently afflicted him; however, afterwards he begged of him that he would leave his last words with him before he died. Then the blessed man Guthlac raised a little his weary limbs from the wall, and thus spake to him: My

bearn, nu ys þære tide swiþe neah, ac behealt þu
min þa ytemestan bebodu.   Æfter þon þe min sawl
of þam lichaman fére, þonne far þu to minre swustor
and hyre secge þæt ic forþon her on middanearde
hire ansyne fleah and hi geséon nolde, þæt wyt eft
on héofonum befóran Godes ánsyne unc eft gesáwon ;
and hi bidde þæt heo minne lichaman on þa þrúh
gesette, and mid þære scytan bewínde þe me
Ecgburh ousende.   Nólde ic þa hwile þe ic leofode
mid línenum hrǽgle gegyred beon, ac nu for lufan
þære Cristes fæmnan, þa gife þe heo me sende ic
wylle to þon dón þe ic heold ; þonne se lichama
and seo sawul hi todǽleð, þæt man þone lichaman
mid þam hrǽgle bewínde, and on þa þruh gelecge.
Ða se foresprecena broðor þas þing gehyrde, he þa
wæs þus sprecende : Ic þe halsige, mín se leofa
fǽder, nu ic þine untrumnysse geseo and ongite,
and ic gehyre þæt þu þas woruld scealt forlǽtan,
þæt þu me secge be þære wisan þe ic nǽfre ǽr næs
gedyrstig þe to axianne.   Of þære tide þe ic ærest
mid þe on þisum westene eardode, ic þe gehyrde
sprecau on æfenne and on æren-mergen ic nat mid
hwæne.   Forþon ic þe bidde and halsige þæt þu
me nǽfre behydigne and sorhfulne be þisse wisan
ne lǽte æfter þinre forðfóre.   He þa se Godes wer
mid langre sworetunge þæt orð of þam breostum
teah, andswarode him þa and cwæð : Min bearn,
nelt þu beon gemyndig, þas þing þe ic ǽr nolde

son, now is it very near the time, and do thou attend to my last commands. After my soul departs from the body, then go thou to my sister, and say to her, that I for this end here on earth avoided her presence and would not see her, that we two hereafter might see each other in heaven, before the face of God; and bid her that she place my body in the coffin, and wind it in the sheet which Ecgburh sent to me. I would not, whilst I lived, be clothed with a linen garment; but now, for love of the maid of Christ, the gift which she sent me I will put to the purpose for which I have kept it, namely, when my body and my soul part, let them wrap my body in the vestment, and lay it in the coffin. When the aforesaid brother heard these things, he thus spake: I beseech thee, my dear father, now while I behold and understand thy infirmity, and I hear that thou must leave this world, that thou explain to me concerning a matter which I never before durst ask thee about. From the time that I first dwelt with thee in this wilderness I have heard thee at even and at daybreak speaking I know not with whom. Wherefore I beg and beseech thee that thou never leave me anxious and troubled about this matter after thy departure. The man of God with a long sigh drew the breath from his breast, answered him and said: My son, be thou not troubled,—the things which before I would tell to

nænigum woruld-men secgan, þa hwile þe ic lifigende
wǽre, ic hit þe wylle nu onwreon and gecyþan.
Ðan æfteran geare þe ic þis westen eardode, þæt on
ǽfen and on ærne-mergen God sylfa þone engcel
mínre frofre to me sende, se me þa heofonlican
gerýno openode, þa nanegum men ne alyfað to
secganne, and þa heardnysse mines gewinnes mid
heofonlican engellicum spræcum ealle gehihte; þe
me æfweardan gecydde and geopenode swa þa andweardan.[1]   And nu mín bearn, þæt leofe, geheald
þu mín word, and þu hi nænigum oþrum men ne
secge buton Pege minre swustor and Ecgberhte
þam ancran, gif þæt gelimpe þæt þu wið hine
gesprece.   Þa he þas word spræc he þa his heafod
to þam wage onhylde, and mid langre sworetunge
þæt orð of þam breostum teah.   Mid þy he eft
gewyrpte, and þam orðe[2] onfeng, þa com seo swetnys
of þam muðc swa þæra wynsumestra[3] blostmena
stenc.   And þa þære æfter-fylgendan nihte mid þan
þe se foresprecena broðor nihtlicum gebedum befeall,
þa geseah he eall þæt hus útan mid mycelre beorht-
nesse ymbsceald; and seo beorhtnys þær áwunode
oð dæg.   Þa hit on mergen dæg wæs, he þa se
Godes wer eft styrede hwæt-hwego and þa weregan
leomu upahof.   Þa cwæð he to him þus: Min
béarn, gearwa þe þæt[4] þu on þone sið fére þe ic þe
gehét; forþon nu ys seo tid þæt se gást sceal for-

---

¹ MS. andweardum.   ² MS. orð.
³ MS. wynsumesta blostman.   ⁴ MS. ⁊

no man of the world while I lived, I will now reveal
and make known to thee. The second year after
I dwelt in this wilderness, at even and at daybreak
God himself sent the angel of my comfort to me,
who opened to me the heavenly mysteries, which it
is lawful to no man to tell, and the hardness of my
conflict he quite softened with heavenly angelic discourses; who also made known and revealed to me
absent as well as present things. And now, my son,
beloved one, keep thou my word, and tell these
things to no other person except to Pege my sister
and to Ecgberht the hermit, if it chance that thou
speak with him. When he had spoken these words,
he leaned his head to the wall, and with a long sigh
drew the breath from his breast. When he turned
himself again and recovered his breath, there came
fragrance from his mouth like the odour of the
sweetest flowers. And on the following night, when
the aforesaid brother fell to his nightly prayers,
he beheld all the house encompassed about with a
great brightness; and this brightness remained
there till day. When it dawned on the morrow,
the man of God stirred again a little, and raised up
his weary limbs. Then spake he thus to him : My
son, prepare thyself to go on the journey which I
bid thee; for now is the time that the spirit must

lætan þa weregan limo and to þam úngeendodan
gefean wyle geferan, to heofona rice.   Ða he þa þas
þingc spræc he þa his handa aþenede to þam weofode,
and hine getrymede mid þam heofonlican mete,
Cristes lichaman and his blode[1]; and þa æfter · þon
his eagan to heofonum ahóf, and his earmas aþenede,
and þa þone gast mid gefean and blisse to þam ecum
gefean sende[2] þæs heofonlican rices.   Betwux þa
þingc se foresprecena broðor geseah eall þæt hus mid
heofonlicre bryhto geond goten, and he þær geseah
fyrenne torr[3] up of þære eorþan to heofones heannysse,
þæs beorhtnys wæs eallum oþrum úngelic, and for his
fægernysse þæt seo sunne sylf æt middum dǽge,
eall hire[4] scima wæs on blæco gecyrred.   And eng-
cellice sangas geond þære lyfte faco he gehyrde;
and eall þæt igland mid mycelre swétnysse wunder-
lices stences ormǽdum wæs gefylled.   He þa se
foresprecena broþor sona mid mycelre fyrhte wæs
geslégen, éode þa on scip and þa ferde to þære stowe
þe se Godes wer ǽr bebead; and þa com to Pege
and hire þa eall þa þing sǽde æfter endebyrdnesse
swa se broðor hine het.   þa heo þa gehyrde þone
broþor forðferedne, heo þa sona on eorðan feoll and
mid mycelre hefignysse gefylled wearð þæt heo word
gecweþan ne mihte.   Mid þan heo þa eft hig gehyrte,
heo þa of þam breostum inneweardum lange sworetunge teah, and þa þam Wealdende þanc sǽde þæs
þe he swá wolde.   Hi þa þan æfteran dǽge æfter

---

[1] MS. blod.   [2] MS. ferde.   [3] MS. fyrene topp.   [4] MS. hira.

leave the weary limbs, and will go to the endless joy, the kingdom of heaven. When he had said these things, he stretched out his hands to the altar, and strengthened himself with the heavenly food, Christ's body and blood. And after that he raised his eyes to heaven, and stretched out his arms, and then sent forth his spirit with joy and bliss to the eternal happiness of the heavenly kingdom. Amidst these things the aforesaid brother saw all the house perfused with heavenly brightness, and he beheld there a fiery tower, from the earth up to the height of heaven, whose brightness was unlike all other, and by its brilliance the sun itself at midday, —all its lustre was turned to paleness. And he heard angelic songs through the regions of the air ; and all the island was profusely filled with the exceeding sweetness of a wondrous odour. Thereupon the aforesaid brother was smitten with great fear, went on board a boat, and travelled to the place which the man of God had before bidden him seek ; and there he came to Pege, and told her all these things in order as her brother had bidden him. When she heard that her brother was departed, she forthwith fell on the earth, and was filled with great sorrow, so that she could not speak a word. When she presently recovered herself, she drew from her breast within a long sigh, and gave thanks to the Lord for that he would have it so to be. Then

þam bebode þæs eadigan weres hi becomon to þam
eglande, and hi ealle þa stowe and þa hus þær gemetton mid ambrósie þære wyrte swetnysse gefylde.
Heo[1] þa þone halgan wer on þreora daga fæce mid
halgum lof-sangum Gode bebead, and on þam þriddan
dæge swa se Godes wer bebead hig þone lichaman
on cyrcan mid arwurðnysse bebyrgdon. Awolde seo
godcunde[2] arfæstnys mannum openlice ætywan on hu
mycclum wuldre he wæs se eadiga wer syþþan he bebyrged wæs; forþon þe he ǽr beforan manna eagum
swá manigum wundrum sceau and berhte.   Mid þy he
þa wæs twelf monað bebyrged æfter his forðfóre, ða
onsende God on þæt mod þære Drihtnes þeowan,
þæt heo wolde eft þone broðorlican lichaman on oðre
byrgene gesettan.   Heo þa þyder togesomnode
Godes þeowa and mæsse-preosta and circlicre[3] endebyrdnysse, þæt þy ylcan dæge þæs ymbe twelf monað
þe seo forðfóre þæs cadigan weres wæs, hi þa þa
byrgene untyndon; þa gemetton hi þone lichaman
ealne ansúndne swa he ǽr wæs and þa gyt lifigende
wǽre, and on liþa[4] bignyssum and on eallum þingum
þæt he wæs slæpendum men gelicra myccle þonne
forðferedum.   Swylce eac þa hrǽgl þære ylcan
niwnysse þe hig on fruman ymbe þone lichaman
gedón wǽron.   þa hi þas þing gesawon þe þér
samod æt wǽron, þa wǽron hi swiðe forhte for þig
þe hi þær gesawon; and hi swa swyðe mid þære

---

[1] MS. IIi.   [2] MS. godcundnysse arfæstlice manna.
[3] MS. cynlice.   [4] MS. liþo.

they on the next day, according to the command of the blessed man, came to the island, and they there found all the place and the buildings filled with the sweetness of the herb ambrosia. She then for three days' space, with holy hymns of praise commended the holy man to God, and on the third day, as the man of God had bidden, they buried the corpse in the church with solemnity. The divine goodness would openly display to men in how great glory the blessed man was after he was buried ; as he erewhile, before the eyes of men, shone and was resplendent with so many miracles. After his death, when he had been buried twelve months, God put it into the heart of the servant of the Lord that she should remove her brother's body to another tomb. She assembled thither many of the servants of God, and mass-priests, and others of ecclesiastical order ; and on the same day, on which, twelve months before, the departure of the blessed man took place, they opened the tomb, and there they found the corpse quite sound as it was at first, and as though he were yet living ; and in the flexibility of the sinews and in all things, it was much more like a sleeping man than a dead one. Also the garments were of the same newness as when they were first put round the body. When they who were there assembled together saw these things, they were much amazed at what they saw ; and they were so smitten with

fyrhtc wǽron geslégene þæt hi naht sprecan ne
mihton. Ða heo þa seo Cristes þeowe Pege þæt
geseah, þa wæs heo sona mid gastlicere blisse gefylled and þa þone halgan lichaman mid þære
arwurðnysse Cristes lof-sangum on oþre scytan be-
wand, þa Ecgbriht se ancra ǽr him lifigende to þære[1]
ylcan þenunge sende. Swylce eac þa þruh na læs
þæt hi eft þa on eorðan dydon, ac on gemyndelicre
stowe and on árwyrþre hi þa gesetton. Seo stow
nu eft fram Aðelbalde þam kyninge mid manigfealdum getimbrum ys arwurðlice gewurþod, þær se
sigefæsta lichama þæs halgan weres gastlice resteþ;
and se man se þe þa stowe mid ealle his mǽgne
geseoð, þonne þurh þa þingunge þæs halgan weres
he gefremeð and þurhtyhþ þæt he wilnað. Se
eadiga wer Guðlac he wæs gecóren man on god-
cundum dǽdum and ealra gesnyttra gold-hord; and
he wæs gestæþþig on his þeawum, swylce he wæs on
Cristes þeowdóme swa geornfullice abysgod þæt him
nǽfre elles on his muðe næs buton Cristes lof, ne
on his heortan butan árfæstnys, ne on his móde
butan syb and lufu and mildheortnes; ne hyne nan
man yrre geseah ne úngeornfulne to Cristes
þeowdome, ac á man mihte on his andwlitan lufe
and sibbe ongytan, and á wæs swetnys on his móde
and snyttro on his breostum and swá mycel
glǽdnys[2] on him wæs, þæt he á þam cuðum and
þam uncuþum wæs gelice gesegen.

---

[1] MS. þam.   [2] MS. glædnysse.

the fear thereof that they could say nothing. But when Pege, the servant of Christ, beheld it, she was forthwith filled with spiritual joy; and she wound the holy corpse, with praises of Christ's honour, in the other sheet which Ecgbriht the anchorite formerly sent him, when alive, for that same service. Also the coffin they did not put into the earth again, but they set it in a memorable place and an honourable. The place has now since then been honourably distinguished by king Athelbald with manifold buildings, where the victorious body of the holy man spiritually rests : and the man who with all his heart seeks that place, through the intercession of the holy man he shall accomplish and bring about what he desires. The blessed man Guthlac was a chosen man in divine deeds, and a treasure of all wisdom; and he was steadfast in his duties, as also he was earnestly intent on Christ's service, so that never was aught else in his mouth but Christ's praise, nor in his heart but virtue, nor in his mind but peace and love and pity; nor did any man ever see him angry nor slothful to Christ's service; but one might ever perceive in his countenance love and peace; and evermore sweetness was in his temper, and wisdom in his breast, and there was so much cheerfulness in him, that he always appeared alike to acquaintances and to strangers.

XXI.

Be Aþelbalde kyningce.

Æfter þyssum geacsode Aþelbald se foresprecena
wræcca on feor-landum þæs halgan weres fórðfóre,
Scc Guþlaces; forþon he ana ǽr þon wæs hys
gebeorh and frofor.   Þa wæs he semninga mid
unrotnysse gestýred, ferde þa þider to þære stowe
þær þæs Godes weres lichama on wæs, forþon he
gehyhte þurh þone halgan wer þæt him God sealde
his gewinnes frofre.   Þa he þa to þære byrgene
com þæs halgan weres, he þa wepende mid tearum
þus cwæð: Mín fǽder hwæt þu canst mine yrmþa,
þu me wǽre symble on fultume on mínum unyð-
nyssum : hwider wylle ic me nu cyrran, hwa frefreð
me gif þu me forlætst?   Mid þy he þa þas þing
and manig oþer æt þære byrgene wepende sprǽc,
þa seo nihtlice tid com, þa wæs he þær on sumum
huse inne þe he ǽr be Guthlace lifigendum hwilum
on gæstliþnesse wunode.   Ða he þa on þam huse
inne wæs, þa wæs he on þam únrotan móde hider
and þyder þencende, him þa æt nyxtan wǽron þa
cagan mid þam slǽpe betyned.   He þa fǽringa
forhtlice abrǽd, þa geseah he ealle þa cytan innan
mid heofonlice leohte gefylde.   Mid þan he þa wæs
forhtlice geworden for þære úngewunelican gesihþe,
ða geseah he þone eadigan wer Guthlac on engellicre ansyne him beforan standan and him cwæð to:

XXI.

Concerning king Athelbald.

After these things Athelbald, the afore-mentioned exile, heard in far lands of the death of the holy man St. Guthlac; for he alone was formerly his refuge and comfort. Then was he suddenly agitated with sorrow, and went thither to the place where the body of God's servant was, for he hoped that through the holy man God would grant him comfort in his conflict. When he came to the tomb of the holy man, weeping with tears, he thus spake: My father, lo! thou knowest my miseries, thou wast ever my support in my afflictions; whither shall I now turn myself; who shall comfort me if thou forsakest me? After he had with weeping said these things and much else at the tomb, when the hour of night came, he was in a house where he had often abode as a guest whilom when Guthlac was living. Whilst he was in this house, whilst he was turning his thoughts hither and thither in his sorrowful mind, his eyes were at length closed in sleep. Suddenly he woke up in a fright, and there he saw all the cottage filled within with heavenly light. Whilst he was in fear at the unusual sight, he saw the blessed man Guthlac in angelic aspect stand before him, and he spake thus to him: Thou shalt

Ne wylt þu þe ondrǽdan, ac beo þu ánræde, forþon
God þe ys on fultume : and ic forþon to þe cóm,
þurh mine þingunge God þine bene gehyrde.   Ac
ne beo þu geunrotsod forþon dagas synt gewitene
þinra yrmða, forþon ǽr sunne twelf monða hringe
útan ymbgán hæbbe þu wealdest þises ríces[1] þe þu
hwile æfter wunne.   And na læs þæt an þæt he him
þæt rice towerd sǽde, ac eac þa lengce his lifes he
him eall gerehte.   Ðas tacna God geworhte þurh
þæs halgan weres geearnunge æfter þon þe he forð-
fered wæs and bebyrged.

XXII.

Wæs sum his scipes-man þæs foresprecenan[2] wræccan
Aþelbaldes on þære mægða Wissa, þæs eagan wǽron
mid fleo and mid dimnesse twelf monð ofergán.
Mid þy his læcas[3] hine mid sealfum lange teolodon,
and hit him nawiht to hǽlo ne fremede ; ða wæs he
innan godcundlice manod þæt gif hine man to þære
stówe gelædde Guthlaces, þæt he þonne his hælo
and gesihþe onfengce.   Næs þa nænig hwil to þon
þæt him his frynd on þǽre stowe brohton to
Cruwlande, and hi þa gesprǽcon to þære Cristes
þeowan Pegan ; and heo þæs mannes geleafan
trumne and fæstne gehyrde.   þa lædde heo hine
on þa cyrcan þær se arwyrða lichama inne wæs

---

[1] MS. rice.   [2] MS. foresprecena.   [3] MS. læces.

not be afraid, but be thou steadfast, for God is thy
support; and I am therefore come to thee, for that
through my intercession God hath heard thy prayer.
But be thou not sorrowful, for the days are past of
thy afflictions; for ere the sun shall have gone a
twelve months' circuit round about, thou shalt
wield this kingdom, which thou erewhile didst con-
tend for. And not only did he prophesy to him
his future kingdom, but he also related to him
completely the length of his life. These signs God
wrought through the holy man's merit after he was
dead and buried.

XXII.

There was a boatman of the aforesaid exile
Athelbald whose eyes had been for twelve months
overspread with the white speck and dimness.
When his physicians had long treated him with
salves, and this no whit effected his healing, he was
divinely admonished within, that if they brought
him to Guthlac's resting-place he should recover
his health and sight. Not long after his friends
brought him to the place Crowland, and they spoke
to Christ's servant Pege; and she was informed of
the firm and fast faith of the man. Then she led
him to the church wherein the venerable body of

Guthlaces ; genam þa þæs gehalgodan sealtes þe
Guthlac ǽr sylf gehalgode, and wætte and drypte
in þa eagan ; and þa ǽr heo oþerne drópan on þæt
oþer eage dyde, þa mihte he mid þan oðrou geseon,
and on þam ylcan inne he géarlice oncneow hwæt
þær inne wæs, and he hal and gesund ham ferde.

Sy urum Drihtne lof and wuldor and wurðmynt,
and þam eadigan were Sce Guthlace on ealra worulda[1]
woruld áá buton ende on ecnysse.   Amen.

---

[1] MS. woruld áworuld.

Guthlac was; she took some of the hallowed salt which Guthlac himself had formerly hallowed, and wetted it, and dropped it on his eyes; and ere she put a second drop on the second eye he was able to see with that eye, and he readily perceived what there was in the room, and he went home whole and sound.

Be praise and glory and honour to our Lord, and to the blessed man St. Guthlac, world of all worlds, for ever and ever, without end to eternity. Amen.

NOTES AND ILLUSTRATIONS.

Page 2. PROLOGUE.

As a specimen of the style of Felix, and to enable the reader to form some judgment of the liberties taken by the Saxon translator, I transcribe the Latin prologue entire.*

✝ Incipit Prologus de vitâ Sci Guthlaci.

In Domino dominorum domino meo. Mihi præ ceteris regalium primatum gradibus dilectissimo, Ælfwaldo regi orientalium Anglorum rite regimina regenti, Felix catholicæ congregationis vernaculus per-petuæ prosperitatis in Christo salutem.

Jussionibus tuis obtemperans libellum, quem de vitâ patris beatæ memoriæ Guthlaci componi præcepisti, simplici verborum vimine textum, non absque procacitatis imprudentiâ, institui: eâ tamen fiduciâ coram obtuli, obsecrans ut si ullatenus, ut fore arbitror. illic vitiosus sermo aures eruditi lectoris perculserit, litteram in fronte paginæ veniam poscentem intendat. Reminiscatur quoque, efflagito, quia regnum Dei non in verborum facundiâ, sed in fidei constantiâ persistit. Salutem quidem sæculo non ab oratoribus sed a piscatoribus prædicatam fuisse sciat. Sancti quoque Hieronimi dicta meminerit, qui rem ridiculam esse arbitratus est, ut sub regulis Donati gram-matici verba cœlestis oraculi redigeret. Sed si forsitan alius animo-sitatis nostræ fastibus hoc opus nos arripere imputat, dum alii plurimi Anglorum librarii, quorum ingeniositatis fluenta inter flores rethoricæ per virecta litteraturæ pure liquide lucideque rivant, qui melius lucu-lentiusque componere valuerint,—sciat nos hoc opusculum non tam

* From the Cotton MS. Nero E. 1, with some corrections from the Benedictine and Bollandine texts.

volentiæ quam obedientiæ gratiâ incepisse. Propterea laboris mei votis, O Lector, quisquis es faveas; sin etiam ut adsolet more obtrectatoris succensueris, cave ut ubi lucem putaveris ne a tenebris obcæceris;—id est, ne cum recta reprehenderis ignorantiæ tenebris fusceris. Mos enim cæcorum est, cum in luce perambulant tunc in tenebris errare putant. Lucem enim nesciunt sed in tenebris semper oberrant. Cæcitas autem in Scripturis ignorantia est, ut apostolus dixit: Cæcitas ex parte contigit in Israel donec plenitudo gentium subintraret. Origo quidem totius mali ab ignorantiâ venit. Quapropter te admoneo, Lector, ut aliena non reprehendas, ne ab aliis quasi alienus reprehendaris. Sed ne sensus legentium prolixæ sententiæ molesta defensio obnubilet, pestiferis obtrectantium incantationibus aures obturantes, velut transvadato vasti gurgitis æquore, ad vitam Sancti Guthlaci stilum flectendo quasi ad portum vitæ pergemus. Quoniam igitur exegisti a me ut de vitâ Sancti Guthlaci vel conversatione tibi scriberem, quemadmodum cœperit quidve ante propositum fuerit vel qualem vitæ terminum habuerit, prout a dictantibus idoneis testibus quos scitis audivi, addendi minuendique modum vitans, eadem orthothemio depinxi; ad hujus utilitatis commodum hunc codicellum fieri ratus, ut illis qui sciunt ad memoriam tanti viri nota revocandi fiat, his vero qui ignorant velut late pansæ viæ indicium notescat. Non enim sine certissimâ inquisitione rerum gestarum aliquid de tanto viro scribebam, nec tandem ea quæ scripsi sine subtilissimâ indubiorum testium sanctione libratim scribenda quibusdam dare præsumpsi; quin potius diligentissime inquirens quantacunque scripsi investigavi a reverendissimo quodam abbate Wilfrido et a presbitero puræ conscientiæ, ut arbitror, Cissan, vel etiam ab aliis qui diutius cum viro Dei conversati vitam ipsius ex parte noverant. Ergo quantacunque de vitæ ipsius orthonomiâ stilo perstrinxero, minima de magnis pauca de plurimis audisse æstimate. Non enim ambigo illos dictatores non omnia facta illius potuisse cognoscere, nec ab illis tota dictata me descripsisse glorifico. Sed ut tanti viri tanti nominis relatio compleatur, prout ubique miracula illius fulserunt, percunctamini, ut singulis quæ novere referentibus sequentis libelli materia adgregetur. Igitur eximiæ dilectionis tuæ imperiis obtemperans, textum præsentis cartulæ prout potui digessi, majoris scientiæ auctoribus majorem partem linquens; principium in principium, finem in fine compono.

Page 2, *line* 3. Alfwold.

Grammatical correctness requires the dative, Alfwolde. The Saxon scribe is often guilty of cutting off an *e*, and as frequently of adding one when not required. To avoid swelling the number of alterations, I suffer Alfwold to stand here, and the reader, if he pleases, may take the word for a vocative.

bid. line 9. Ahtest.

Literally, Thou didst own. This can hardly be the true reading: Qu.? Tæhtest, *præcepisti*.

Ibid. þære arwurðan gemynde.

The MS. has, þæs arwurðan gemynde, which I have altered as above, because in the two other places in which the phrase occurs in the Life of Guthlac, as well as in numerous instances in Alfred's Beda, such is the form of the expression. In p. 20, l. 9, we have, Mid þan se foresprecena wer and þære eadigan gemynde Guthlac, etc.; and p. 24, l. 22, Swa þonne þære arwurðan gemynde Guðlac .... wæs gelæd, etc. In Beda, lib. iv, cap. xxiii (p. 593, l. 4, Smith), To lare þære eadigan gemynde Paulinus, þæs ærestan biscopes Norþanhymbra, etc.; and ib. p. 594, l. 18, Cwom þa to Cent to ðære cadigan gemynde Theodore ærcebiscope. See also lib. iv, cap. xxviii, (p. 606, l. 46); and lib. iv, cap. xix, (p. 587, l. 27).

The idiom is remarkable in two points: 1, for the use of gemynd in the feminine gender; and 2, for the agreement of the definite article with a word to which it does not properly belong, by the process expressively named, Attraction.

1. In Ælfric's Homilies, gemynd is used constantly as a neuter (or possibly masculine; as the oblique cases, which occur the most frequently, do not determine whether the word be masculine or neuter). Bosworth considers it masculine. But in Hom. vol. i, p. 288, þæt gemynd occurs several times. In Alfred's Beda the usage is commonly the same. One instance I have remarked of seo gemynd (lib. v, cap. vii, near the end); a stricter search may perhaps yield more.

2. The phrase, þære cadigan gemynde wer, is a substitute for se

wer eadiges gemyndes (or, eadigre gemynde). A transposition taking place of the qualitative genitive and the noun qualified, we should obtain, Se eadigre gemynde wer. But the article being attracted by the substantive with which it is now in juxtaposition, the ear triumphing over logic, the phrase becomes, þære eadigan gemynde wer. This process is very different from that which takes place when a *possessive* genitive is placed before the noun it defines. For instance, þæt heafud þæs horses, properly becomes, þæs horses heafod. Here it will be observed, that the genitive, having an article of its own, naturally retains it on changing its position, the other noun dropping its article, which becomes superfluous. If, however, the genitive be a word which does not admit of, or at any rate has not, the definite article, then the principal noun retains its article unchanged; e. g. for þæt word Godes, we find, þæt Godes word (Matt. xii, 20); for þære lufan Godes, þære Godes lufan (Guthl. p. 16, l. 14); and, se Godes man, seo Cristes fæmne, are expressions of constant occurrence. So Beda, lib. iii, cap. ii, (p. 536, l. 18,) þære wæpned-manna stowe, the men's apartment. Perhaps, however, in some of these cases, the genitive may be more properly considered as one of qualification than of possession; and words thus connected may be looked upon as compounds, the latter word merging that which precedes, so that the intervening genitive leaves the concord of the article with its noun undisturbed.

The following are instances of the change of the article by *attraction:* Luke xvi, 8; þære unrihtwisnesse tun-gerefan, instead of, þone tun-gerefan unrihtwisnesse, the steward of unrighteousness, i. e. the unrighteous steward. John xvi, 13; þære soðfæstnysse Gast, instead of, þone Gast soðfæstnysse, the Spirit of truth.

Page 2, *line* 14. [wordum].

The whole of this passage is very corrupt. Without emendation it yields no sense at all. The insertion and alterations which I have made, make it agree in some measure with the original. The words, ac gemune and geþence, are repeated apparently by mistake; fram idelum þaucum, must be wrong; but whether the mistake be that of the translator or the scribe, I cannot determine, and leave the words as I find them.

Page 4, *line* 1. swa ic menige, etc.

The translator has departed entirely from the original, and it is not easy to tell exactly what he means. The order of the sentence appears to be inverted; gegylde and gesette agreeing, as I believe, with boc;—fægere and glæwlice gesette, could hardly be said of the writers of books. As a similar instance of inversion, compare p. 14, l. 20, þa caldan kyningas, ... þurh earmlicne deað and þurh sarlicne utgang þæs mánfullan lifes, þe þas woruld forleton.

Ibid. line 27. þæt him þonne, etc.

See Vernon's Guide to the Anglo-Saxon Tongue, p. 86, for similar constructions. An instance occurs, p. 16, l. 13, barn him swa swyþe innan þære Godes lufan.

Page 6, *line* 3. geradne.

Gerad, means *apt, suited, well-calculated;* from rædan. The sense of the modern German, gerade, i. e. straight, seems appropriate in this place.

Ibid. line 7. Ne tweoge ic aht, etc.

It will be perceived that the Saxon version expresses exactly the opposite of the meaning of the original. The insertion of a negative, ne, before mihton, would remedy this; but the latter part of the paragraph does not seem to favour the alteration.

Ibid. line 13. hyrde.

This word, which answers to cartulæ in the Latin, is not found in the dictionaries. Can it be an error of the copyist for hyde? Is that word ever used in the sense of a parchment or skin for writing? The passage is probably corrupt; and moreover the translator seems to have quite mistaken the sense of the original, as the reader will see by comparison.

Page 8, *line* 1. Æþelredes.

Æthelred began to reign A.D. 675, resigned his throne A.D. 704, and died A.D. 716. See Mr. Thorpe's Translation of Lappenberg's History of the Anglo-Saxon Kings, vol. i, p. 222 ; and the table of the kings of Mercia, at the end of the volume.

According to the Saxon Chronicle, Guthlac died A.D. 714. Felix says, anno 715 ab incarnatione Domini ; a reckoning commencing nine months before the birth of our Lord. This date may therefore be considered to correspond with that of the Chronicle. According to Felix, St. Guthlac was twenty-six years old when he settled at Crowland, and resided there fifteen years ; he must therefore have been forty-one or forty-two, at the time of his death. This brings his birth back to 673 or 672, and therefore before the commencement of Æthelred's reign.

Ibid. line 2. heh-þeode.

Latin : De egregia Merciorum stirpe. Does heh-þeod mean rather the principal or royal family of Mercia ? But compare p. 66, l. 7, where it must needs be rendered, province.

Ibid. line 4. Iclingas.

The sixth in descent from Woden, in the genealogy of the kings of Mercia, was Icel, from whom this family took its name.

Ibid. line 8. þa ana.

Qu. ? Should we read þa anan, or ane. In the sense of *alone*, ana is used as an accusative ; e. g. Hom. i, p. 184, Me ána forlæt, leave me alone ; and p. 350, Min latteow me þær ána forlet, my guide left me there alone.

Ibid. line 15. mid inseglum.

Did the termination *um* originally characterize the dative or ablative *singular* of substantives as well as of adjectives ? There is no sense of plurality in such expressions as : on swefnum (see Matt. ii, 22), in a dream ; to gemyndum, to remembrance ; on hys gewealdum, in his power ; be lyfum, alive ; and many like phrases. It is usual to term *um*, in these instances, an adverbial termination ; but I see nothing to distinguish it in the examples adduced from a regular case-ending.

Page 10, *line* 3. þa com sum wif . . . yrnan.

In Anglo-Saxon, after verbs expressing *motion,* or the absence of it, the infinitive is required, where in modern English a present, in German a past, participle is used. Thus, *A.-S.* he com yrnan ; *Germ.* er kam gerannt ; *Eng.* he came running.

For instances, see p. 30, l. 16, þa comon twegen deoflu of þære lyfte slidan ; p. 40, l. 26, þa geseah he þær standan twegen þara awerigdra gasta wepan (MS. weopon) swyþe and geomerian.

In the poetical Legend of St. Guthlac, Cod. Ex. 179, 4 ff.

ða cwom leohta mæst.

halig of heofonum.

hædre scinan.

In the poem of the Phœnix, Cod. Ex. p. 204, 5 ff.

hwonne up cyme.

æþelast tungla.

ofer yð-mere.

estan lixan.

Ibid. line 9. forþon þe þæt bearn þær acenned wæs.

There is some defect in the Anglo-Saxon version here. The Latin is as follows : Alii vero hæc audientes, ex divino præsagio ad manifestandam nascentis gloriam illud fuisse perhibebant. Alii autem sagacioris sententiæ conjecturis promere cœperunt hunc ex divinâ dispensatione in perpetuæ beatitudinis præmia destinatum esse.

Ibid. line 20. of þære þeode Guþlac.

Latin : Ex appellatione illius tribus quam dicunt Guthlacingas, proprietatis vocabulum ex cœlesti consilio, Guthlacus, percepit, quod ex qualitatis compositione consequentibus meritis conveniebat. Nam ut illius gentis gnari perhibent Anglorum linguâ hoc nomen ex duobus integris constare videtur, hoc est *Guth* et *lac.*

This passage seems to indicate that the author, Felix, was not an Englishman. The MS. has, feawum gewritum ; a mistake, it is to be hoped, of the copyist. I have merely substituted twam for feawum, but suspect that error still lurks in gewritum. Gewrit signifies rather a sentence, or inscription, than a single term.

Page 10, *line* 24. forþon þeah.

Perhaps þeah is merely an error of the scribe for þe.   I have translated the passage as if þeah .... þeah, were equivalent to cum .... cum,
for which, þe .... þe is commonly used in Anglo-Saxon.   The Latin
runs thus :   Quia ille cum vitiis bellando æternæ beatitudinis præmia
cum triumphali infula perennis vitæ percepisset.   The Saxon translator has apparently taken *cum* for a conjunction.   There is a passage
in Cædmon where þeah appears to be used like þe; p. 34, l. 2 (Thorpe's
edition) :

> nát þeah þu mid ligenum fáre.
>
> þe þu drihtnes eart.
>
> boda of heofonum.

" I know not whether thou comest with lies, or whether," etc.

Page 12, *line* 20.   Ac on his scearpnysse þæt he weox.

An ellipsis of the words ða wæs or ða gelamp, must be supposed to
take place here, to account for the use of the particle of dependence,
þæt.   Instances of this are frequent in the Life of Guthlac, e. g.
p. 24, l. 17, ff., He wæs ær-þon ehtere his þære halgan cyrcan, and
mid þan þe he to Damascum ferde þære byrig, þæt he wæs of þam
þystrum gedwolum abroden, etc.; p. 18, l. 18, Da ymbe twá winter
þæs þe he his lif swa leofode under munuchade, þæt he þa ongan, etc.

Ibid. ult. he þa, swa he of slæpe onwoce, wearð his mot oncyrred.

An instance of anacoluthon, or change of construction ; mod is the
nominative to wearð, and he, the principal nominative in the sentence,
is left without a verb.   So p. 88, l. 13, And for his fægernysse
þæt seo sunne sylf æt middum dǽge, eall hire scima wæs on blæco
gecyrred.

Page 14, *line* 14.   wealcan dwelode.

The passage corresponding to this in the original is as follows
Inter dubios volventis temporis eventus et atras caliginosæ vitæ ne-
bulas, fluctuantisque *sæculi gurgites jactaretur.*   The words in italics
are those of which only a translation is attempted in the Anglo-Saxon
The MS. reads weolc ꝸ welode.   Weolc. perf. from wealcan is explained

by Bosworth (who refers to this passage), revolvit, effervescebat; and welode (which he identifies with wellode fr. wellian), æstuavit. That the passage is corrupt appears, I think, from this, that betweox requires an accusative or a dative (Vernon, p. 89), and such word must immediately follow middan-cardes. By the alteration of one letter, and a distribution of those contained in ꝺ (and), a reading is obtained which at least presents less difficulty than that of the MS., and is nearer to the Latin. Wealcan may be either the dative pl. from wealc, for wealcum, or possibly the infinitive of the verb, wealcan, used as a substantive, according to the German usage. I am not, however, prepared to adduce instances of this use of the infinitive.

Ibid. line 19. ff.

The original runs thus : Nam cum antiquorum regum stirpis suæ per transacta sæcula miserabiles exitus et flagitiosum vitæ terminum contemplaretur, necnon et caducas mundi divitias contemptibilemque temporalis vitæ gloriam pervigili mente consideraret, tunc sibi proprii obitus sui imaginatam formam osteudit, etc. I have translated the passage, under the impression that allusion was made to the numerous nstances of Saxon kings who forsook their thrones to become monks ir anchorites; a practice which came into fashion in Guthlac's time. The sense of the Latin is however different; and it may be perhaps better to translate: " who departed this world, by a miserable death and a wretched ending of their sinful life."

Page 16, line 20.   Hrypadún.

Repton, in Derbyshire, once famous for its monastery, and as the capital city and burial-place of the kings of Mercia.

Page 18, line 20.   wilnian westenes and sundor-setle.

Qu.? whether we should read sundor-setles. Perhaps, however, the habitual dislike of uniformity which displays itself in the Anglo-Saxon spelling, may be traced in this junction of two different cases with the same verb. (Wilnian generally requires a genitive, or a dative preceded by the preposition, on or to.) As instances of a similar usage, compare Ælf. Hom. vol. ii. p. 604, gelyfan on þa Halgan Ðrynnysse and soðre Annysse ; Luke viii. 34, on þa ceastre and on tunum.

Page 20, *line* 9. Se foresprecena wer and þære eadigan gemynde Guðlac.

The use of two articles coupled by a conjunction, to indicate one and the same object, is worthy of notice. For a similar instance, see Beda, lib. iv, cap. xxvii (p. 603, l. 26), Mon þone halgan wer and þone arwurþan Cuþbyrht to biscope gehalgode.

Ibid. line 14, þære stowe digelnysse.

The MS. reads þa stowe digelnysse. But as this expression must be considered as equivalent to þa digelnysse þære stowe, I have no hesitation in altering þa to þære, in conformity with the principle alluded to in the note on p. 2, l. 9.

Ibid. line 26. eahtoða dæg.

In the original, die nono Kalendarum Septembrium; i. e. the 24th of August.

Page 24, *line* 12. sceotode.

Sceotian, to shoot, a transitive verb, from sccotan, sceat, sentou, scoten, intransitive; a distinction which has been lost in modern English. So hangian, to hang, transitive, from hon (hangan), heng, hangen, intransitive. See p. 50, l. 16, 17.

Page 26, *line* 4. Wæs þær on þam calande, etc.

The Vercelli Fragment begins here abruptly. Wæs þær in þam sprecenan iglande sum mycel hlæw of corþan geworht, þone ylcan hlæw iu geara men bræccou and dulfon for feoc [r. feos] þingum, etc.

Ibid. line 11.

Verc. Fr. Ða þohte he þæt he nawðer þara, etc.

Ibid. line 13.

Verc. Fr. ealle dagas his lifes.

Page 26, *line* 14.

Verc. Fr. he hit swa forð-gelæste.

Ibid. line 15.

Verc. Fr. wæs his ondleofones swylc gemetegung. This last word I have adopted in the text, instead of the Cottonian reading, to gereorde, which does not agree with the original, and is tautologous.

· *Ibid. line* 20.

Verc. Fr. mid þy he þy gewunelican þeowdome his sealmas sang and his gebedum ætfealh, þa se ealda feond mancynnes gengde geond þæt græs-wang, swa grymetende leo, þæt he his costunga attor wide geond stregde.

Page 28, *line* 1.

The remainder of this sentence is very carelessly written in the Vercelli Fragment; the reader may find some exercise for his ingenuity in correcting it. Mid þy he þa yfelnes mægen and his grimnesse attor teldað [r. todæleð], þæt he mid þy atre þa menniscan heortan wundað, þa semninga swa he of bendum and of brogan wæs his cos-tunga ða he ða þam earh winnendan stræle on þam mode gefæstnode þæs Cristes cempan.

The words earh winnendan are apparently a gloss carelessly in-serted in the wrong place; perhaps we should read þam earh-winnendan mode, the faintly striving soul. Earh, substantive, means an arrow; but I do not see how that sense can be given to it here. The Latin runs thus: Dum enim omnis nequitiæ suæ vires versuta mente ten-taret, tum veluti ab extenso arcu venenifluam desperationis sagittam totis viribus jaculavit, quousque in Christi militis mente umbone defixa pependit.

Ibid. line 5.

Verc. Fr. werigan for awerigedan. The same substitution takes place wherever the word occurs.

Ibid. line 10.

Verc. Fr. fyrena for synna.

Page 28, *line* 18.

Verc. Fr. wol-berendan for tweogendum.

Page 30, *line* 1.

Verc. Fr. feonde for bliþe.

Ibid. line 7.

Verc. Fr. hine het þæt him ne tweode no, etc.

Ibid. line 9.

Verc. Fr. ða he se haliga Guðlac þæs word gehyrde his þæs ge-
trywan freondes, þa wæs he on gæstlicre blisse and heofoncundre
gife swiðe ḡfeode [r. gefeonde] and his geleafan fæste in God sylfne
getrymede and fæstnode. Syððan seo tid wæs þæt næfre þæt deoful
eft wið hine þære ormodnesse wæpnum on hine sceotode.

Ibid. line 16.

Verc. Fr. tu for twegen.

Ibid. line 20.

Verc. Fr. cunedon for fandedon.

Ibid. line 21.

Verc. Fr. ussa for ure.

Ibid. line 22.

Verc. Fr. Wene ic [r. is] þæt we þe furðor ne wyllan leng swencan
ne ðe mid brogan bysmrian, &c.

Page 32, *line* 3.

Verc. Fr. middangeardes for middaneardes.

Ibid. line 8, ff.

Verc. Fr. Þonne gif þu þæs wilnast þæt þu of ðe ða ærian fre-
mednesse yfelra leahtra of-aðwea, þonne scealt þu þinne lichaman

þurh forhæfednesse weccean, forþan swiððor swa ðu þe her on worulde wecst [qu.? swencst] and weccest to forgifenesse þinra gylta swa ðu þonne eft bist in ecnessum getrymed fæstlicor, and swa micle swiðor swa ðu on þyssan andweardan life ma earfeða dreogest swa micle þu eft in towyrdnesse forgifest, and þanne þu bist on fæsten her on worulde astreaht, þonne bist þu ahafen for Godes eagan.

Page 32, line 18.

Verc. Fr. swa on teala micelre, etc.

Ibid. line 19.

Verc. Fr. bið to clænsigeanne se man.

Page 34, line 1.

Verc. Fr. geþence for oncnawe.

Ibid. line 3.

Verc. Fr. rec for smic.

Ibid. line 5, ff.

Verc. Fr. hie þa ealle idle and unnytte ongeat; ac þa feng to þære teala myclan andleofone, þæt wæs to þam berenan hlafe, and þone geþygde and his feorh bigferede.

Ibid. line 10.

Verc. Fr. mid wependre stefne bemurnon and wide geond þæt land waðdon; and he se geadiga wer swa gesigefæsted þa bysmornesse ealle forhogode þæra werigra gasta and him for-naht dyde.

The verb waðan, to wander, flee, is not in Bosworth.

Ibid. line 18.

Verc. Fr. cyrme for cyme.

Ibid. line 19. Hi wæron, etc.

This description has been somewhat abridged by the Anglo-Saxon translator: I give it in full, marking in italics the parts omitted in the translation.

Erant enim aspectu truces, *formâ terribiles*, capitibus magnis, collis longis, macilentâ facie, lurido vultu, squallidâ barbâ, auribus hispidis, fronte torvâ, trucibus oculis, ore fœtido, dentibus equinis, gutture flammivomo, *faucibus tortis*, *labro lato*, vocibus horrisonis, *comis combustis, buccula crassá, pectore arduo, femoribus scabris*, genibus nodosis, cruribus nucis, talo tumido, plantis aversis, *ore patulo*, clamoribus raucisonis. Ita enim immensis vagitibus horrescere audiebantur, ut totam pæne a cœlo in terram intercapedinem clangisonis boatibus implerent.

The Vercelli Fragment agrees in these omissions, which is sufficient to show that it is based upon the same text as the Cotton MS., notwithstanding the material alterations introduced throughout.

Page 34, line 20.

Verc. Fr. lange for langne.

Ibid. line 21.

The word manigre (Verc. Fr. mænigre) I have replaced by mægere, in accordance with the original, macilentâ.

Ibid. line 22. orfyrme.

From or, privative, and feormian, to cleanse. Verc. Fr. bearde for beardum.

Ibid. line 23.

Verc. Fr. egeslice eagan and ondrysenlice muðas, and heora teð wæron horses tuxum gelice, and him wæron þa hracan lige afylled. Toþas (in the text) for teð is worthy of note. The same form occurs in the poetical dialogue of Saturn and Solomon, line 230. In Cod. Ex. 219, 1. 22, fotas is used for fét.

Page 36, line 1.

Cott. MS. mís crocetton. Verc. Fr. misscrence tán. The latter reading I adopt in the text. Bosworth explains mis-crocetton, croaked badly. This does not come very near the original, ore patulo; and the reading misscrence tán answers much better to the words plantis aversis. Gescrencean, for-screncan, mean to trip up, supplantare.

Ælfric uses the word for-screncend to explain the name Jacob, i. e. supplanter. Hom. vol. i, p. 586. Gescrincan, forscrincan, from which these words are derivatives, mean to *shrink*, wither, intransitively. Mis-screnc (qu.? mis-screnct) may therefore well mean distorted, shrivelled.

Page 36, line 2.

Verc. Fr. and hi swa ungemetlice hrymdon and foran mid forht-licum egesum and ungeþwærnessum þæt hit þuhte þæt hit eall be-tweoh, etc.

Ibid. line 5.

Verc. Fr. ylding for yldend. The termination *end* denotes an actor, *ing* or *ung*, an action. The words, Næs þa nænig yldend must there-fore be explained to mean, None of them delayed; not, There was no delay.

Ibid. line 7.

Verc. Fr. gebundenum hine tugon.

Ibid. line 9.

Verc. Fr. þæt swearte fenn.

Ibid. line 9.

The Cotton MS. reads orwehtan, which Bosworth explains, without water (from or, and, wæt). The original is, cœnosis. The reading of the Verc. Fr. horwihtan, from horu, horuwe, filth, mud (like stæmiht, hæriht), seems clearly the true one, and I have adopted it in the text.

Ibid. line 12.

Verc. Fr. betuh for betwux.

Ibid. line 14.

Verc. Fr. on þære þystran nihte.

Ibid. line 15.

Verc. Fr. Læton hie hine bidan ana and gestandan.

Page 36, *line* 17.

Verc. Fr. Mid maran brogan bysmrigan and wǽcan.

Ibid. line 21.

Verc. Fr. omits the words fram þe, which come in awkwardly enough in the text.

Ibid. line 24.

Verc. Fr. in þam ondrysenlicum fiðerum betuh þa caldan facu.

Ibid. line 27.

Verc. Fr. þam sweartestum afylled swiðra genipa. Þa geseah he semninga þær ða ondrysenlican fiðeru ongen cuman þara werigra gasta, and unmæte weorod hyra þær coman togenes.

Page 38, *line* 2.

Verc. Fr. geþyddon for gegaderodon.

Ibid. line 4.

Verc. Fr. tintreges gomum helle dures. The Cottonian MS. reads duru, which, if retained, must be considered, I suppose, as an accusative. The passage seems to require the dative, and I have accordingly placed dura in the text. If dures be not a mere blunder of the scribes, it adds another anomaly to the declension of duru, which is properly decl. III. 3 of Rask, but takes dura and duran in the oblique cases.

Ibid. line 4.

Verc. Fr. Ða he ðær geseah þa smicendan þismas (qu. ? þrosmas) þara byrnenda liga, and þone ege þære sweartan nywylnesse, he ða sona wæs ofergeotol ealra þæra tintrega þe he fram þam werigum gastum ær dreah and drefde; and na læs þán (r. þæt an) þæt he þær þa leglican hyðe ðæs fyres upþyddan geseah and eac þa (r. þæs) fullan swefles þær gescah upgeotan.

To these latter words there is no equivalent in the Cottonian MS. They correspond, however, to a paragraph in the original.

Page 38, *line* 9.

Verc. Fr. ligeas for lega.

Ibid. line 13.

Verc. Fr. þara wita, and hine for þy ege swiðlice onþræc, ða cleopodon, etc.

Ibid. line 16.

Verc. Fr. on ðæs witu þisse neowolnesse.

Ibid. line 20.

Verc. Fr. þystra bearnum and forwyrde tuddor, ge syndon dustes acsan : hwa geaf eow yrmingum, etc.

Ibid. line 24.

Verc. Fr. earo for gearu.

Ibid. line 26.

Verc. Fr. bregian for egsian.

Page 40, *line* 5.

˙ Verc. Fr. betuh þa dimman þystro. The Cottonian text has þa dimnysse þeostru. Dimnysse, a genitive of quality, intervenes between the substantive and its article, in place of an adjective, without disturbing the concord. See Note on p. 2, l. 9.

Ibid. line 7.

Verc. Fr. gewunigean for awunian.

Ibid. line 8.

Verc. Fr. hie sylfe in heolstre hydden.

Page 40, *line* 10.

Verc. Fr. gefeannesse for gefean. The Fragment winds up here with the words : And þa æfter þam fleah se haliga Guðlac mid þam Apostole Sce Bartbolomei to heofona rices wuldre, and hine se Hælend þær onfeng, and he þær leofað and rixad in heofona rices wuldre a butan ende on ecnesse. Amen, fiat.

Ibid. line 21. Ibnut de virtute, etc.

These were the words which Furseus heard chanted by the angelic host. I refer the reader to Mr. Wright's interesting work entitled, St. Patrick's Purgatory, for an account of the visions of that saint, and others of a similar character, which belong to the age of Guthlac.

Page 42, *line* 7.

Cenred began to reign A. D. 704, and in A.D. 709 went to Rome, where he ended his days.

Ibid. line 20. afyldon.

The original runs : Illum vero intercipientes, acutis hastarum spiculis in auras levare cœperunt. I am doubtful whether afyldon should be translated " they filled" or " they felled," but have adopted the latter meaning.

Page 44, *line* 22. þwean.

It may be proper to observe that the original has nothing equivalent to the words, þæt he hine wolde þwean, which would seem to imply that Guthlac's ablutions took place only every twenty days. The Latin is : Ut assolebat, post bis denos dierum cursus *tonderare* devenisset.

Page 46, *line* 6. þa deaþ-berendan wæter.

Several neuters of the third declension in *el, en, er, or,* which should regularly form their nominative and accusative plural in *u,* are found occasionally (as if belonging to the second declension), making no alteration in these cases. See p. 36, l. 9, þa horwihtan wæter. Beda, p. 690, l. 10 (Smith), þa wundor. Orosius, lib. iv, cap. 2, þa yfelan wundor.

Life of Guthlac, p. 72, l. 3, þa wundor. Cod. Ex., p. 111, l. 15, þurh gastlicu wundor. Beda, p. 608, l. 39, call þa hrægel . . . ungewemmed wæron; and p. 609, l. 10, þa sylfan hrægel. Life of Guthlac, p. 90, l. 23, þa hrægl. Cod. Ex., p. 204, l. 12, tungol beoð ahyded. Cod. Ex., p. 20, l. 11, beoð wolcen towegen.

Page 46, *line* 10. unablinnu.

Bosworth explains this word to mean incessatio, non intermissa series, from blin or ablinnan. The Latin text has no word corresponding to it. It seems to belong to the class of neuter plurals used in an abstract sense, like eaðmetto and ofermetto. (Rask, Gram. 92.)

Ibid. *line* 20. befeal.

This is the perfect of a verb, befeolan, which is not given in Bosworth's Lexicon, but which occurs infra, p. 52, ult. Ætfeolan, perf. ætfealh is given in the Lexicons, and the Vercelli Fragment uses this word for befeal, p. 26, l. 21. There appears to be two distinct verbs, namely, feallan, p. feoll. part. gefeallan (conj. ii, 2, of Rask); and feolan, p. feal or fealh (qu.? iii, 1, making, perhaps, folgen in the participle). As the Anglo-Saxon does not form one verb of the complex order from another of the same, I question whether there be any radical connexion between these verbs; and would suggest, as matter for inquiry, whether the verb fyligean or fylgan (conj. ii, 2, the *g* being a radical letter) be not derived from feolan, fealh. (See Rask, Gram. 347.) The *h* in the perfect points to a *g* in the root. Befeolan, ætfeolan, answer to the words incumbere, insistere, and involve the idea of *pursuing* rather than *falling*.

Page 50, *line* 8. sarig.

Grammar requires sarigne. It is difficult to say whether a reading of this kind is the result of mere carelessness in transcription, or of lax and corrupt usage. In p. 92, l. 22, we find: Ne hyne nan man yrre geseah ne úngeornfulne, etc., where yrrne would be grammatically correct.

Ibid. *line* 14. þæt egland.

Qu.? þæm eglande. Neah governs the dative. In p. 58, l. 19, we find, wel neah þam eglande.

Page 50, *line* 20.

Qu. ? whether we should not read gearnunge, and mildheortnysse, according to the Latin construction; non sui meriti, sed divinæ miserationis. However, in p. 58, l. 16, we find: Gif þæt Godes stihtung wære, which may support the use of the nominative in this passage.

Ibid. line 10. gefere.

Properly gefera; and in the title we should read geferan. The word is of Decl. i, 2, of Rask. I abstain from correcting in the text, thinking that this spelling may be not so much an error of the scribe as a corrupt usage, occasioned by the existence of a numerous class of words in *ere* (Decl. ii, 2), to which gefere may have been thought to belong. In the title of chap. xviii, Hædde is written for Hæddan, and in that of chap. xvii, abbodysse for abbodyssan. The latter I have corrected in the text.

Page 52, *line* 4. leofe-bene.

Leof, læf or leaf, *leave.* Hence leafe-ben, leave-asking.

Ibid. line 9. drencton.

MS. dremdon. If this reading be retained, translate, "they delighted each other." The original is, Divinarum Scriptuarum haustibus inebriarent; from which, and from the similar use of indrencton, p. 72, l. 7, I have little doubt drencton is the true reading.

Page 54, *line* 22. þæs huses hrofe.

The MS. has þam. As a particular house is meant, it is to the word huses that the article must belong, and I correct accordingly. See Note on p. 2, l. 9.

Page 56, *line* 2. mid bliðum andwlite and góde mode.

I have before noticed the use of two different cases with one preposition. Here we have the dative and ablative joined with mid.

Page 58, *line* 5. acsodon.

The verb acsian, like the Greek πυνθάνομαι, means to receive information as well as to demand it. See p. 94, l. 1.

Page 60, *line* 6. raxende.

This word is not to be found in Bosworth, nor in any of the Anglo-Saxon glossaries which I have consulted. The Latin runs thus : Ipse autem, velut qui de æstuantis gurgitis fluctibus ad portum deducitur, longa suspicia imo de pectore trahens, etc. To these latter words raxende appears to correspond. The word raxed occurs in Piers Ploughman, explained by Mr. Wright in the glossary, To hawk, spit. Raux, or rax, is also a north-country word, signifying to stretch (see Jameson's Scottish Dictionary, and Halliwell's Dictionary of Archaic and Provincial Words), probably akin to the Anglo-Saxon ræcan, reach, retch.

Page 64, *line* 23. behydde.

For behyddon. It is not noticed in the grammars that the perfect (as well as the present, see Rask, Gram. 197) frequently takes the termination *e* for *on* in the plural, when the pronoun follows the verb. As instances, take the following : Matt. vii, 22, Hú ne witegode we on þinum naman ? Matt. xii, 3, Ne rædde ge ? Matt. xxiii. 31, gyf we wæron on ure fædera dagum, nære we geferan. Matt. xxvi, 37, Hwænne gesawe we ? John xv, 16, ne gecure ge me. Ælf. Hom. vol. ii, p. 350, l. 5, Ða become wit to anre dene.

Page 66, *line* 11. aþer oððe.

A similar redundancy of the disjunctive aþer occurs in Alfred's Orosius (Thorpe's Analecta, p. 84) : Eall þæt his man aþer oððe ettan oððe erian mæg.

Page 68, *line* 17. hine.

Reaf being neuter, if this reading be correct, we must suppose hine to refer to some masculine noun signifying a garment ; gegyrla, perhaps.

Ibid. line 23. on þa fyrle.

German : in die ferne, into the distance.

Page 72, *line* 14. [bysena.]

Latin : Divinarum scripturarum exemplis.

6

Page 74, *line* 1. þam biscopes þegnum.

I have abstained from correcting, but have little doubt that the true reading is þæs biscopes þegnum, the officers of a particular bishop being meant, not bishop's-officers, as we say sheriff's-officers, indicating a distinct class of persons. In p. 70, l. 12, we find, correctly, þæs bisceopes þegnas.

Ibid. line 3. hwylc þincð.

MS. þince, in the subjunctive. But it does not seem correct to use the subjunctive after a direct interrogative. If the words saga me precede, so as to make the interrogative dependent, the Anglo-Saxon permits either the indicative or subjunctive to follow. The dialogues of Salomon and Saturn, and of Adrian and Ritheus, afford numerous examples of this varying usage. In the latter dialogue, Question 24, Saga me, hwylce wihta beoð, etc.; and Question 28, Saga me, hwylc man wære deád, etc.

Page 74, *line* 10. hárfæstlice.

MS. árfæstlice. Latin : In autumnali tempore.

Ibid. line 14. Aldwulfes.

Aldwulf, king of the East-Angles, began to reign A.D. 663, died A.D. 713. His daughter Ecgburh was abbess of Repandun. See Genealogy of the Kings of East-Anglia, Thorpe's Lappenberg, vol. i.

Page 76, *line* 13. Ceolred.

Began to reign A.D. 709, died A.D. 716. Æthelbald, the exile here mentioned, succeeded him in A.D. 716. See Genealogy of the Kings of Mercia, Thorpe's Lappenberg, vol. i.

Page 78, *line* 5. on gerisne.

Dr. Bosworth translates this phrase rapinâ, from risan or gerisan, to seize. The original certainly is : Non in prædâ, nec in rapinâ regnum tibi dabitur. But qu.? whether it be not from gerisen, fit, right ; meaning jure or ratione, by right, or, in consequence of. Compare the phrases mid rihte and mid gerisenum, coupled in p. 2, l. 4.

Page 78, *line* 12. þæt ricu, etc.

In the original these words commence the next chapter, and are preparatory to the account of Guthlac's death. Verum quoniam humanum genus ab initio mortalis miseriæ quotidie ad finem decurrit, mutatis temporibus generationes et regna mutantur, etc. A line has apparently been lost in the translation, wherein mention was made of the human race, to which hit is meant to refer. But compare p. 86, l. 2.

Ibid. line 13. se rica, etc.

These nominatives want a verb, the construction being changed, as in p. 88, ll. 13, 14.

Page 80, *line* 2. hine het gyrwan.

Latin: præparare cœpit. Literally, he bid himself prepare.

Page 80, *line* 21. mettrumnys.

MS. mettrumnysse. The termination nysse for nys in the nominative occurs so frequently in the MS. hereabouts, that it may be thought to be less the blunder of the copyist than an evidence of declining attention to correctness of grammatical inflexion at the time when he wrote. Smith's Beda affords numerous instances of the same corruption.

Page 82, *line* 4. eago-spind.

Literally, eye-fat. The glossaries spell this word in a great variety of ways. Hagu-spind, hagu-swind, eagan-spind, eagan-swind, heago-spind, hecga-spind.

Ibid. line 10.

The original has: Tantæ ergo fidei fuit, ut mortem quæ cunctis mortalibus timenda formidandaque videtur, ille velut requiem aut præmium laboris judicaret. The words se cuþa, etc., seem introduced by mistake, and afford no sense. A phrase somewhat similar occurs p. 92, ult., where the original is: Ita ut extra humanam naturam notis ignotisque esse videretur.

Page 84, *line* 1. behealt.

So the MS. Beheald is the correct reading. Syut occurs for synd, p. 96, l. 4, perhaps indicating that the final *d* (as in modern German) often assumed the sound of *t*.

Ibid. line 7. bidde.

More correctly, bide. Rask, Gram. 230.

Ibid. ult. nelt.

Wyllan has no imperative mood; because, as Ælfric the grammarian observes, the will should ever be free. It is in accordance with this rule that we find nelt and ne wylt (p. 96, l. 1), the 2d person present indicative, used instead of an imperative. Yet as the will may be controlled, a real imperative (nelle) of the negative verb nyllan is also admitted. So in Latin, noli; there being no corresponding imperative to volo.

Page 86, *line* 8. gehihte.

Hiht means hope, joy; hence gehihtan must mean here to alleviate by inspiring hope.

Page 88, *line* 11. torr.

MS. topp, i. e. vertex, fastigium. The Latin has turrim; and in the metrical version, Cod. Ex. p. 180, l. 26, the word used is tor.

> Heofonlic leoma.
> from foldan up.
> swylce fyren tor.
> ryht aræred.

Ibid. line 17. ormædum.

Qu.? ormætum.

Page 90, *line* 7. Awolde, etc.

A very similar passage occurs in Alfred's Beda, lib. iv, cap. 30, by the help of which we may correct the errors of the text in this place. Wolde ða openlicor ætywan seo godcunde arfæstnysse (read arfæstnys) on hu myclum wuldre se Drihtnes wer Cuþbyrht æfter his deaþe lifede, ðæs his lif ær þam deaþe mid healicum tacnum heofonlicra wundra openode and ætywde.

Ibid. line 16. circlicre.

MS, cynlice.   Latin : aliis ecclesiasticis gradibus.

Page 96, *line* 12. his scipes-man.

Latin : quidam vir paterfamilias in provinciâ Wissa, without any mention of Athelbald.   Probably the true reading is hiwscipes-man, and the words, þæs foresprecenan wræccan Aþelbaldes, should be omitted.

Ibid. line 13.   Wissa.

The province of the Gewissas or West Saxons, I presume.   See Thorpe's Lappenberg, vol. i, p. 109.

Ibid. line 14. fleo.

Latin : albugo.   A white spot in the eye.   Written also fleah. Somner gives the word eag-flea, in the same sense.

FINIS.

C. AND J. ADLARD, PRINTERS, BARTHOLOMEW CLOSE.

VALUABLE AND INTERESTING BOOKS,

PUBLISHED OR SOLD BY

JOHN RUSSELL SMITH,

4, OLD COMPTON STREET, SOHO SQUARE, LONDON.

𝕻𝖍𝖎𝖑𝖔𝖑𝖔𝖌𝖞 𝖆𝖓𝖉 𝕰𝖆𝖗𝖑𝖞 𝕰𝖓𝖌𝖑𝖎𝖘𝖍 𝕷𝖎𝖙𝖊𝖗𝖆𝖙𝖚𝖗𝖊.

A Dictionary of Archaic and Provincial Words,

Obsolete Phrases, Proverbs, and Ancient Customs, from the Reign of Edward I. by JAMES ORCHARD HALLIWELL, F.R.S., F.S.A., &c. 2 vols. 8vo. containing upwards of 1000 pages, *closely printed in double columns, cloth,* £2. 2s

This work, which has occupied the Editor some years, is now completed; it contains above 50,000 words (embodying all the known scattered glossaries of the English language) forming a complete key for the reader of the works of our old Poets, Dramatists, Theologians, and other authors whose works abound with allusions, of which explanations are not to be found in ordinary Dictionaries and books of reference. Most of the principal Archaisms are illustrated by examples selected from early inedited MSS. and rare books, and by far the greater portion will be found to be original authorities.

Guide to the Anglo-Saxon Tongue: on the Basis

of Professor Rask's Grammar, to which are added Reading Lessons in Verse and Prose, with Notes for the use of Learners, by E. J. VERNON, B.A., Oxon. 12mo. *cloth,* 5s 6d

"The author of this Guide seems to have made one step in the right direction, by compiling what may be pronounced the best work on the subject hitherto published in England."—*Athenæum.*

"Mr. Vernon has, we think, acted wisely in taking Rask for his model; but let no one suppose from the title that the book is merely a compilation from the work of that philologist. The accidence is abridged from Rask, with constant revision, correction, and modification; but the syntax, a most important portion of the book, is original, and is compiled with great care and skill; and the latter half of the volume consists of a well-chosen selection of extracts from Anglo-Saxon writers, in prose and verse, for the practice of the student, who will find great assistance in reading them from the grammatical notes with which they are accompanied, and from the glossary which follows them. This volume, well studied, will enable any one to read with ease the generality of Anglo-Saxon writers; and its cheapness places it within the reach of every class. It has our hearty recommendation."—*Literary Gazette.*

The Anglo-Saxon Version of the Life of St. Guth-

lac, Hermit of Croyland. Printed for the first time, from a MS. in the Cottonian Library, with a Translation and Notes by CHARLES WYCLIFFE GOODWIN, M.A., Fellow of Catharine Hall, Cambridge, 12mo. *cloth,* 5s

An Introduction to Anglo-Saxon Reading; com-

prising Ælfric's Homily on the Birthday of St. Gregory, with a copious Glossary, &c. by L. LANGLEY, F.L.S. 12mo. *cloth,* 2s 6d

Compendious Anglo-Saxon and English Dictionary,

by the Rev. JOSEPH BOSWORTH, D.D., F.R.S., F.S.A., &c.—*Will be ready very shortly.*

It will contain all the words of the large octavo edition, with numerous additions, and will be published at a price which will place it within the reach of all who take an interest in the language of their forefathers.

Reliquiæ Antiquæ.—Scraps from Ancient Manu-
scripts, illustrating chiefly Early English Literature, and the English Language, edited by WRIGHT and HALLIWELL, 2 vols. 8vo. *cloth, £2. 2s*— *reduced to £1. 4s*

Containing communications by Ellis, Madden, Hunter, Bruce, Turnbull, Laing, Nichols, &c. But very few copies remain. Odd numbers may be had to complete sets at 2s. each.
It contains a large number of pieces in Anglo-Saxon, Anglo-Norman, and Early English ; it will be found of use to future Philologists, and to all who take an interest in the history of our language and literature.

Popular Treatises on Science, written during the
Middle Ages, in Anglo-Saxon, Anglo-Norman, and English, 8vo. edited by THOS. WRIGHT, *cloth, 4s 6d*

Contents :—An Anglo-Saxon Treatise on Astronomy of the TENTH CENTURY, *now first published from a MS. in the British Museum, with a translation ;* Livre des Creatures, by Phillippe de Thaun, *now first printed with a translation, (extremely valuable to the Philologist, as being the earliest specimens of Anglo-Norman remaining, and explanatory of all the symbolical signs in early sculpture and painting) ;* the Bestiary of Phillippe de Thaun, *with a translation ;* Fragments on Popular Science from the Early English Metrical Lives of the Saints, (*the earliest piece of the kind in the English language.*)

Anecdota Literaria : A Collection of Short Poems
in English, Latin, and French, illustrative of the Literature and History of England in the XIIIth Century ; and more especially of the Condition and Manners of the different Classes of Society, by T. WRIGHT, M.A., F.S.A., &c. 8vo. *cloth, only* 250 *printed, 7s 6d*

Philological Proofs of the original Unity and recent
Origin of the Human Race, derived from a Comparison of the Languages of Asia, Europe, Africa, and America, by A. J. JOHNES, 8vo. [*cloth, reduced from* 12s 6d *to* 6s

Printed at the suggestion of Dr. Pritchard, to whose works it will be found a useful supplement.

Early Mysteries, and other Latin Poems of the
XIIth and XIIIth centuries, edited from original MSS. in the British Museum, and the Libraries of Oxford, Cambridge, Paris, and Vienna, by THOS. WRIGHT, M.A., F.S.A., 8vo. *bds. 4s 6d*

" Besides the curious specimens of the dramatic style of Middle-Age Latinity, Mr. Wright has given two compositions in the Narrative Elegiac Verse (a favourite measure at that period), in the Comœdia Babionis and the Geta of Vitalis Blesensis, which form a link of connexion between the Classical and Middle-age Literature ; some remarkable Satyrical Rhymes on the people of Norfolk, written by a Monk of Peterborough, and answered in the same style by John of St. Omer; and lastly, some sprightly and often graceful songs, from a MS. in the Arundel Collection, which afford a very favourable idea of the Lyric Poetry of our clerical forefathers."—*Gentleman's Mag.*

An Essay on the Origin, Progress, and Decline of
·Rhyming Latin Verse, with many specimens, by Sir ALEX. CROKE, post 8vo. *cloth, 7s 6d*—*reduced to 3s*

" This is a clever and interesting little volume on an attractive subject, the leisure work of a scholar and man of taste."—*British Critic.*

On the Origin and Formation of the Romance Lan-
guages; containing an examination of M. Raynouard's Theory on the Relation of the Italian, Spanish, Provençal, and French, to the Latin, by GEO. CORNEWALL LEWIS, 8vo. *cloth, 12s—reduced to 7s 6d*

Essays on the Literature, Popular Superstitions,

and History of England in the MIDDLE AGES, by THOMAS WRIGHT, M.A., F.S.A., 2 stout vols. post 8vo. *elegantly printed, cloth,* 16s

Contents :—Essay I. Anglo-Saxon Poetry. II. Anglo-Norman Poetry. III. Chansons de Geste, or Historical Romances of the Middle Ages. IV. On Proverbs and Popular Sayings. V. On the Anglo-Latin Poets of the Twelfth Century. VI. Abelard and the Scholastic Philosophy. VII. On Dr. Grimm's German Mythology. VIII. On the National Fairy Mythology of England. IX. On the Popular Superstitions of Modern Greece. and their connection with the English. X. On Friar Rush, and the Frolicsome Elves. XI. On Dunlop's History of Fiction. XII. On the History and Transmission of Popular Stories. XIII. On the Poetry of History. XIV. Adventures of Hereward the Saxon. XV. The Story of Eustace the Monk. XVI. The History of Fulke Fitzwarine. XVII. On the Popular Cycle of Robin-Hood Ballads. XVIII. On the Conquest of Ireland by the Anglo-Normans. XIX. On Old English Political Songs. XX. On the Scottish Poet Dunbar.

The Early History of Freemasonry in England,

Illustrated by an English Poem of the XIVth Century, with Notes, by J. O. HALLIWELL, post 8vo. SECOND EDITION, *with a facsimile of the original MS. in the British Museum, cloth,* 2s 6d

"The interest which the curious poem of which this publication is chiefly composed has excited, is proved by the fact of its having been translated into German, and of it having reached a second edition, which is not common with such publications. Mr. Halliwell has carefully revised the new edition, and increased its utility by the addition of a complete and correct glossary."—*Literary Gazette.*

Torrent of Portugal; an English Metrical Ro-

mance, *now first published,* from an unique MS. of the XVth century, preserved in the Chetham Library at Manchester, edited by J. O. HALLIWELL, &c. post 8vo. *cloth, uniform with Ritson, Weber, and Ellis's publications,* 5s

"This is a valuable and interesting addition to our list of early English metrical romances, and an indispensable companion to the collections of Ritson, Weber, and Ellis."—*Literary Gazette.*

"A literary curiosity, and one both welcome and serviceable to the lover of black-letter lore. Though the obsoleteness of the style may occasion sad stumbling to a modern reader, yet the class to which it rightly belongs will value it accordingly; both because it is curious in its details, and possesses philological importance. To the general reader it presents one feature, viz. the reference to Wayland Smith, whom Sir W. Scott has invested with so much interest."—*Metropolitan Magazine.*

The Harrowing of Hell, a Miracle Play, written in

the Reign of Edward II., now first published from the Original in the British Museum, with a Modern Reading, Introduction, and Notes, by JAMES ORCHARD HALLIWELL, Esq. F.R.S., F.S.A., &c. 8vo. *sewed,* 2s

This curious piece is supposed to be the earliest specimen of dramatic composition in the English Language ; *vide* Hallam's Literature of Europe, Vol. I. ; Strutt's Manners and Customs, Vol. II. ; Warton's English Poetry ; Sharon Turner's England; Collier's History of English Dramatic Poetry, Vol. II. p. 213. *All these writers refer to the Manuscript.*

Nugæ Poeticæ ; Select Pieces of Old English

Popular Poetry, illustrating the Manners and Arts of the XVth Century, edited by J. O. HALLIWELL, post 8vo. *only 100 copies printed, cloth,* 5s

Contents :—Colyn Blowbol's Testament; the Debate of the Carpenter's Tools ; the Merchant and his Son ; the Maid and the Magpie ; Elegy on Lobe, Henry VIIIth's Fool ; Romance of Robert of Sicily, *and five other curious pieces of the same kind.*

Reliques of Irish Jacobite Poetry, with Interlinear

Translations, and Biographical Sketches of the Authors, and Notes by J. DALY, also English Metrical Versions by E. WALSH, 8vo. parts 1 and 2, (all yet published,) 2s

Rara Mathematica ; or a Collection of Treatises on

the Mathematics and Subjects connected with them, from ancient inedited MSS. by J. O. HALLIWELL, 8vo. SECOND EDITION, cloth, 3*s* 6*d*

Contents: Johannis de Sacro-Bosco Tractatus de Arte Numerandi ; Method used in England in the Fifteenth Century for taking the Altitude of a Steeple; Treatise on the Numeration of Algorism; Treatise on Glasses for Optical Purposes, by W. Bourne; Johannis Robyns de Cometis Commentaria ; Two Tables showing the time of High Water at London Bridge, and the Duration of Moonlight, from a MS. of the Thirteenth Century ; on the Mensuration of Heights and Distances ; Alexandri de Villa Dei Carmen de Algorismo; Preface to a Calendar or Almanack for 1430 ; Johannis Norfolk in Artem progressionis summula ; Notes on Early Almanacs, by the Editor, &c. &c.

Popular Errors in English Grammar, particularly

in Pronunciation, familiarly pointed out, by GEORGE JACKSON, 12mo. Third Edition, *with a coloured frontispiece of the " Sedes Busbeiana,"* 6*d*

Provincial Dialects of England.

Bibliographical List of all the Works which have

been published towards illustrating the Provincial Dialects of England, by JOHN RUSSELL SMITH, post 8vo. 1*s*

" Very serviceable to such as prosecute the study of our provincial dialects, or are collecting works on that curious subject. We very cordially recomment it to notice."
Metropolitan.

An Historical Sketch of the Provincial Dialects

of England, illustrated by numerous examples, Extracted from the " Dictionary of Archaic and Provincial Words," by JAMES ORCHARD HALLIWELL, 8vo. *sewed*, 2*s*

Poems of Rural Life, in the Dorset Dialect, with a

Dissertation and Glossary, by WILLIAM BARNES, SECOND EDITION, ENLARGED AND CORRECTED, royal 12mo. *cloth,* 10*s*

A fine poetic feeling is displayed through the various pieces in this volume; according to some critics nothing has appeared equal to it since the time of Burns ; the ' Gentleman's Magazine' for Dec, 1844, gave a review of the first edition some pages in length.

A Glossary of Provincial Words and Phrases in use

in Wiltshire, showing their Derivation in numerous instances from the Language of the Anglo-Saxons, by JOHN YONGE AKERMAN, Esq. F.S.A., 12mo. *cloth,* 3*s*

The Vocabulary of East Anglia, an attempt to

record the vulgar tongue of the twin sister Counties, *Norfolk and Suffolk,* as it existed in the last twenty years of the Eighteenth Century, and still exists ; with proof of its antiquity from Etymology and Authority, by the Rev. R. FORBY, 2 vols. post 8vo. *cloth,* 12*s* (original price £1. 1*s*)

Westmoreland and Cumberland Dialects, Dialogues,

Poems, Songs, and Ballads, by various Writers, in the Westmoreland and Cumberland Dialects, now first collected, to which is added, a Copious Glossary of Words peculiar to those Counties, post 8vo. pp. 408, *cloth,* 9*s*

This collection comprises, in the *Westmoreland Dialect,* Mrs. Ann Wheeler's Four Familiar Dialogues, with Poems. &c. ; and in the *Cumberlands Dialect,* I. Poems and Pastorals by the Rev. Josiah Relph ; II. Pastorals, &c., by Ewan Clark; III. Letters from Dublin by a young Borrowdale Shepherd, by Isaac Ritson; IV. Poems by John Stagg ; V. Poems by Mark Lonsdale; VI. Ballads and Songs by Robert Anderson, the Cumbrian Bard (*including some now first printed*); VII. Songs by Miss Blamire and Miss Gilpin; VIII. Songs by John Rayson ; IX. An Extensive Glossary of Westmoreland and Cumberland Words.

Specimens of Cornish Provincial Dialects, collected

and arranged by Uncle Jan Treenoodle, with some Introductory Remarks and a Glossary by an Antiquarian Friend, also a Selection of Songs and other Pieces connected with Cornwall, post 8vo. *with curious portrait of Dolly Pentreath, cloth,* 4s

Exmoor Scolding and Courtship in the Propriety

and Decency of Exmoor (Devonshire) Language, *with Notes and a Glossary,* post 8vo. 12th edition, 1s 6d

"A very rich bit of West of Englandism."—*Metropolitan.*

The Yorkshire Dialect, exemplified in various Dia-

logues, Tales, and Songs, applicable to the County, with a Glossary, post 8vo. 1s

"A shilling book worth its money; most of the pieces of composition are not only harmless, but good and pretty. The eclogue on the death of ' Awd Daisy," an outworn horse, is an outpouring of some of the best feelings of the rustic mind; and the addresses to riches and poverty have much of the freedom and spirit of Burns."

Gent.'s Magazine, May, 1841.

A Collection of Fugitive Pieces in the Dialect of

Zummerzet, edited by J. O. HALLIWELL, post 8vo. *only 50 printed,* 2s

Dick and Sal, or Jack and Joan's Fair, a Doggrel

Poem, in the Kentish Dialect, 3rd edition, 12mo. 6d

Jan Cladpole's Trip to 'Merricur in Search for Dollar

Trees, and how he got rich enough to beg his way home ! written in Sussex Doggerel, 12mo. 6d

John Noakes and Mary Styles, a Poem, *exhibiting*

some of the most striking lingual *localisms peculiar to Essex,* with a Glossary, by CHARLES CLARK, Esq. of Great Totham Hall, Essex, post 8vo. *cloth,* 2s

"The poem possesses considerable humour."—*Tait's Mag.*" A very pleasant trifle." *Lit. Gaz.* " A very clever production."—*Essex Lit. Journal.* Full of rich humour."— *Essex Mercury.* "Very droll."—*Metropolitan.* "Exhibits the dialect of Essex perfectly."—*Eclectic Review.* " Full of quaint wit and humour."—*Gent.'s Mag. May* 1841. " A very clever and amusing piece of local description."—*Archæologist.*

Grose's (Francis, F.S.A.) Glossary of Provincial

and Local Words used in England, with which is now first incorporated the SUPPLEMENT by SAMUEL PEGGE, F.S.A., post 8vo. *elegantly printed, cloth,* 4s 6d

The utility of a Provincial Glossary to all persons desirous of understanding our ancient Poets is so universally acknowledged, that to enter into a proof of it would be entirely a work of supererogation. Grose and Pegge are constantly referred to in Todd's " Johnson's Dictionary."

𝔄𝔯𝔠𝔥𝔞𝔢𝔬𝔩𝔬𝔤𝔶 𝔞𝔫𝔡 𝔑𝔲𝔪𝔦𝔰𝔪𝔞𝔱𝔦𝔠𝔰.

The Druidical Temples of the County of Wilts, by

the Rev. E. DUKE, M.A., F.S.A., Member of the Archæological Institute, &c., Author of the " Hall of John Halle," and other works, 12mo. *plates, cloth,* 5s

" Mr. Duke has been long honourably known as a zealous cultivator of our local antiquities. His collections on this subject, and on the literature of Wiltshire, are nowhere surpassed; while his residence on the borders of the Plain, and within reach of our most interesting remains, has afforded scope to his meritorious exertions. The work before us is the fruit of long study and laborious investigation."—*Salisbury Journal.*

An Archæological Index to Remains of Antiquity

of the Celtic, Romano-British and Anglo-Saxon Periods, by JOHN YONGE AKERMAN, F.S.A., in 1 vol. 8vo. *illustrated with numerous engravings, comprising upward of five hundred objects, cloth,* 15s

This work, though intended as an introduction and a guide to the study of our early antiquities, will it is hoped also prove of service, as a book of reference to the practised Archæologist. The contents are as follows:

PART I. CELTIC PERIOD.—Tumuli, or Barrows and Cairns.—Cromlechs.—Sepulchral Caves.—Rocking Stones.—Stone Circles, etc. etc.—Objects discovered in Celtic Sepulchres. —Urns.—Beads.—Weapons.—Implements, etc.

PART II. ROMANO-BRITISH PERIOD.—Tumuli of the Roman-British Period.— Burial Places of the Romans.—Pavements.—Camps.—Villas.—Sepulchral Monuments. —Sepulchral Inscriptions.— Dedicatory Inscriptions. — Commemorative Inscriptions.— Altars.—Urns.— Glass Vessels.—Fibulæ.—Armillæ.—Coins.—Coin-Moulds, etc. etc.

PART III. ANGLO-SAXON PERIOD.—Tumuli.—Detailed List of Objects discovered in Anglo-Saxon Barrows.—Urns.—Swords.—Spears.—Knives.— Umbones of Shields.— Buckles.— Fibulæ.—Bullæ.— Hair Pins —Beads, etc. etc. etc. etc.

The ITINERARY of ANTONINUS (as far as relates to Britain). The Geographical Tables of PTOLEMY, the NOTITIA, and the ITINERARY of RICHARD of CIRENCESTER, together with a classified Index of the contents of the ARCHÆOLOGIA (Vols. i. to xxxi.) are given in an Appendix.

Vestiges of the Antiquities of Derbyshire, and the

Sepulchral Usages of its Inhabitants, from the most remote ages to the Reformation, by THOMAS BATEMAN, Esq. of Yolgrave, 8vo. *profusely illustrated with woodcuts, cloth,* £1. 1s

Notitia Britanniæ, or an Inquiry concerning the

Localities, Habits, Condition, and Progressive Civilization of the Aborigines of Britain ; to which is appended a brief Retrospect of the Results of their Intercourse with the Romans, by W. D. SAULL, F.S.A., F.G.S., &c. 8vo. *engravings,* 3s 6d

A Verbatim Report of the Proceedings at a Special

General Meeting of the British Archæological Association, held at the Theatre of the Western Library Institution, 5th March, 1845, T. J. Pettigrew in the Chair. With an Introduction by THOMAS WRIGHT, 8vo. *sewed,* 1s 6d

A succinct history of the division between the Archæological Association and Institute.

British Archæological Association.—A Report of

the Proceedings and Excursions of the Members of the British Archæological Association, at the Canterbury Session, Sept. 1844, by A. J. DUNKIN, thick 8vo. *with many engravings, cloth,* £1. 1s

" The volume contains most of the papers entire that were read at the Meeting, and revised by the authors. It will become a scarce book as only 120 were printed ; and it forms the first yearly volume of the Archæological Association, or the Archæological Institute."

Coins of the Romans relating to Britain, Described

and Illustrated, by J. Y. AKERMAN, F.S.A., Secretary to the Numismatic Society, &c. Second edition, greatly enlarged, 8vo. *with plates and woodcuts,* 10s 6d

The " Prix de Numismatique" has just been awarded by the French Institute to the author for this work.

" Mr. Akerman's volume contains a notice of every known variety, with copious illustrations, and is published at very moderate price; it should be consulted, not merely for these particular coins, but also for facts most valuable to all who are interested in the Romano-British history."—*Archæological Journal.*

Ancient Coins of Cities and Princes, Geographically

arranged and described, HISPANIA, GALLIA, BRITANNIA, by J. Y. AKERMAN, F.S.A., 8vo. *with engravings of many hundred coins from actual examples, cloth,* 18s

Numismatic Illustrations of the Narrative Portions

of the New Testament, *fine paper, numerous woodcuts from the original coins in various pub*lic *and private* collections, 1 vol. 8vo. *cloth*, 5s 6d

Lectures on the Coinage of the Greeks and Romans,

delivered in the University of Oxford, by Edward Cardwell, D.D., Principal of St. Alban's Hall, and Professor of Ancient History, 8vo. *cloth, reduced from 8s 6d to 4s*

A very interesting historical volume, and written in a pleasing and popular manner.

Essay on the Numismatic History of the Ancient

Kingdom of the East Angles, by D. H. Haigh, royal 8vo. 5 *plates, containing numerous figures of coins, sewed, 6s*

A Hand-Book of English Coins, from the Conquest

to Victoria, by L. Jewitt, 12mo. 11 *plates, cloth*, 1s

Heraldry and Topography.

The Curiosities of Heraldry, with Illustrations from

Old English Writers, by Mark Antony Lower, Author of " Essays on English Surnames;" *with Illuminated Title-page, and numerous engravings from designs by the Author*, 8vo. cloth, Gules, *appropriately ornamented,* or, 14s

"The present volume is truly a worthy sequel (to the 'Surnames') in the same curious and antiquarian line, blending with remarkable facts and intelligence, such a fund of amusing anecdote and illustration, that the reader is almost surprised to find that he has learnt so much, whilst he appeared to be pursuing mere entertainment. The text is so pleasing that we scarcely dream of its sterling value; and it seems as if, in unison with the woodcuts, which so cleverly explain its points and adorn its various topics, the whole design were intended for a relaxation from study, rather than an ample exposition of an extraordinary and universal custom, which produced the most important effect upon the minds and habits of mankind."—*Literary Gazette.*

"Mr. Lower's work is both curious and instructive, while the manner of its treatment is so inviting and popular, that the subject to which it refers, which many have hitherto had too good reason to consider meagre and unprofitable, assumes, under the hands of the writer, the novelty of fiction with the importance of historical truth."—*Athenæum.*

English Surnames. A Series of Essays on Family

Nomenclature, Historical, Etymological, and Humorous; with Chapters on Canting Arms, Rebuses, and the Roll of Battel Abbey, a List of Latinized Surnames, &c. by Mark Antony Lower. The *second edition, enlarged,* post 8vo. pp. 292, *with 20 woodcuts, cloth,* 6s

To those who are curious about their patronymic, it will be found a very instructive and amusing volume — mingling wit and pleasantry, with antiquarian research and historical interest.

An Index to the Pedigrees and Arms, contained

in the Heralds' Visitations, in the British Museum, alphabetically arranged in Counties, 8vo. *cloth,* 10s 6d

An indispensable work to those engaged in Genealogical and Topographical pursuits, affording a ready clue to the Pedigrees and Arms of nearly 20,000 of the Gentry of England, their Residences, &c. (distinguishing the different families of the same name in any county), as recorded by the Heralds in their Visitations between the years 1528 to 1686.

History and Antiquities of the Ancient Port and

Town of Rye in Sussex, compiled from Original Documents, by William Holloway, Esq., thick 8vo. only 200 printed, *cloth,* £1. 1s

Historia Collegii Jesu Cantabrigiensis à J. SHER
MANNO, olim præs. ejusdem Collegii. Edita J. O. HALLIWELL, 8vo. *cloth,*

History and Antiquities of the Hundred of Comp
ton, Berks, with Dissertations on the Roman Station of Calleva Attr
batum, and the Battle of Ashdown, by W. HEWITT, Jun. 8vo. 18 *plate*
cloth.   Only 250 printed, 15s—*reduced to* 9s

Newcastle Tracts; Reprints of Rare and Curiou
Tracts, chiefly illustrative of the History of the Northern Counties; *beaut*
fully printed in crown 8vo. *on a fine thick paper, with facsimile Title*
and other features characteristic of the originals.   Only 100 *copies printe*
Nos. I. to XLIX. £5. 5s
Purchasers are expected to take the succeeding Tracts as published; the Series is near
completed.

A Journey to Beresford Hall, in Derbyshire, th
Seat of CHARLES COTTON, Esq. the celebrated Author and Angler, by W
ALEXANDER, F.S.A., F.L.S., late Keeper of the Prints in the Britis
Museum, crown 4to. *printed on tinted paper, with a spirited frontispiec*
representing Walton and his adopted Son Cotton in the Fishing-house, an
vignette title-page, cloth, 5s
Dedicated to the Anglers of Great Britain and the various Walton and Cotton Club
only 100 printed.

𝕭iography, 𝕷iterary 𝕳istory, and 𝕮riticism.

A New Life of Shakespeare, founded upon recentl
discovered Documents, by JAMES ORCHARD HALLIWELL, F.R.S., F.S.A
with numerous illustrations of objects never before engraved, from drau
ings by F. W. FAIRHOLT, F.S.A., in 1 vol. 8vo. *cloth,* 12s

An Introduction to Shakespeare's Midsumme
Night's Dream, by J. O. HALLIWELL, 8vo. *cloth* (250 *printed*), 3s

An Account of the only known Manuscript o
Shakspeare's Plays, comprising some important variations and correction
in the Merry Wives of Windsor, obtained from a Playhouse copy of th
Play recently discovered, by J. O. HALLIWELL, 8vo. *sewed,* 1s

On the Character of Falstaff, as originally exhibite
by Shakespeare in the two parts of King Henry IV., by J. O. HALLIWEL
12mo. *cloth, (only* 100 *printed,)* 2s

Shakesperiana, a Catalogue of the Early Editions o
Shakespeare's Plays, and of the Commentaries and other Publications illus
trative of his Works, by J. O. HALLIWELL, 8vo. *cloth,* 3s
" Indispensable to everybody who wishes to carry on any inquiries connected wit
Shakspeare, or who may have a fancy for Shakespearian Bibliography."—*Spectator.*

England's Worthies, under whom all the Civi
and Bloody Warres, since Anno 1642 to Anno 1647, are related, by JOH
VICARS, Author of " England's Parliamentary Chronicle," &c. &c. roy
12mo. *reprinted in the old style, (similar to Lady Willoughby's Diary*
with copies of the 18 *rare portraits after Hollar, &c. half morocco,* 5s
Copies of the original edition have been sold from £16. to £20.
The portraits comprise, Robert, Earl of Essex; Robert, Earl of Warwick; Lord Mo
tagu, Earl of Denbigh, Earl of Stamford, David Lesley, General Fairfax, Sir Thomas Fai
fax, O. Cromwell, Skippon, Colonel Massey, Sir W. Brereton, Sir W. Waller, Colon
Langhorne, General Poyntz, Sir Thos. Middleton, General Brown, and General Mitton.

Autobiography of Joseph Lister, of Bradford, in

Yorkshire, to which is added a contemporary account of the Defence of Bradford, and Capture of Leeds by the Parliamentarians in 1642, edited by Thomas Wright, 8vo. only 250 copies printed, *cloth*, 4s

Love Letters of Mrs. Piozzi, written when she was

Eighty, to the handsome Actor, William Augustus Conway, aged Twenty-seven, 8vo. *sewed*, 2s

" —— written at three, four, and five o'clock (in the morning) by an Octogenary pen, a heart (as Mrs. Lee says) twenty-six years old, and as H. L. P. feels it to be, *all your own.*"—*Letter V. 3rd Feb.* 1820.

Collection of Letters on Scientific Subjects, illustra-

tive of the Progress of Science in England temp. Elizabeth to Charles II. edited by J. O. Halliwell, 8vo. *cloth*, 3s

Comprising letters of Digges, Dee, Tycho Brahe, Lower, Harriott, Lydyat, Sir W. Petty, Sir C. Cavendish, Brancker, Pell, &c.; also the autobiography of Sir Samuel Morland, from a MS. in Lambeth Palace, Nat. Tarpoley's Corrector Analyticus, &c. Cost the Subscribers £1.

A Rot among the Bishops; or a Terrible *Tempest*

in the *Sea* of Canterbury, set forth in lively emblems to please the judicious Reader, by Thomas Stirry, 1641, 18mo. (*a satire on Abp. Laud,*) *four very curious woodcut emblems*, *cloth*, 3s

A facsimile of the very rare original edition, which sold at Bindley's sale for £13.

Bibliotheca Madrigaliana.—A Bibliographical Ac-

count of the Musical and Poetical Works published in England during the Sixteenth and Seventeenth Centuries, under the titles of Madrigals, Ballets, Ayres, Canzonets, &c. &c. by Edward F. Rimbault, LL.D., F.S.A., 8vo. *cloth*, 5s

It records a class of books left undescribed by Ames, Herbert, and Dibdin, and furnishes a most valuable Catalogue of the Lyrical Poetry of the age to which it refers.

Who was " Jack Wilson" the Singer of Shake-

speare's Stage ? An attempt to prove the identity of this person with John Wilson, Dr. of Musick in the University of Oxford, A.D. 1644, by E. F. Rimbault, LL.D. 8vo. 1s

𝔓𝔬𝔭𝔲𝔩𝔞𝔯 𝔓𝔬𝔢𝔱𝔯𝔶, 𝔖𝔱𝔬𝔯𝔦𝔢𝔰, 𝔞𝔫𝔡 𝔖𝔲𝔭𝔢𝔯𝔰𝔱𝔦𝔱𝔦𝔬𝔫𝔰.

The Nursery Rhymes of England, collected chiefly

from Oral Tradition, edited by J. O. Halliwell. The Fourth Edition, enlarged, with 38 Designs by W. B. Scott, *Director of the School of Design, Newcastle-on-Tyne,* 12mo. *in very richly illuminated cloth, gilt leaves,* 4s 6d

" Illustrations! And here they are ; clever pictures, which the three-year olds understand before their A, B, C, and which the fifty-three-year olds like almost as well as the threes."—*Literary Gazette.*

" We are persuaded that the very rudest of these Jingles, tales, and rhymes, possess a strong imagination-nourishing power; and that in infancy and early childhood a sprinkling of ancient nursery lore is worth whole cartloads of the wise saws and modern instances which are now as duly and carefully concocted by experienced litterateurs, into instructive tales for the *spelling* public, as are works of entertainment for the reading public. The work is worthy of the attention of the popular antiquary."—*Tait's Mag.*

Wonderful Discovery of the Witchcrafts of Margaret

and Philip Flower, daughters of Joan Flower, near Bever (Belvoir), executed at Lincoln for confessing themselves actors in the destruction of Lord Rosse, son of the Earl of Rutland, 1618, 8vo. 1s

One of the most extraordinary cases of Witchcraft on record.

Saint   Patrick's   Purgatory ;   an   Essay   on   th
Legends of Hell, Purgatory, and Paradise, current during the Middle Age.
by THOMAS WRIGHT, M.A., F.S.A., &c. post 8vo. *cloth*, 6*s*
" It must be observed that this is not a mere account of St. Patrick's Purgatory, but
complete history of the legends and superstitions relating to the subject, from the earlie
times, rescued from old MSS. as well as from old printed books. Moreover, it embraces
singular chapter of literary history, omitted by Warton and all former writers with whor
we are acquainted ; and we think we may add, that it forms the best introduction to Dant
that has yet been published."—*Literary Gazette.*
" This appears to be a curious and even amusing book on the singular subject of Pu
gatory, in which the idle and fearful dreams of superstition are shown to be first narrate
as tales, and then applied as means of deducing the moral character of the age in whic
they prevailed."—*Spectator.*

Trial of the Witches at Bury St. Edmunds, befor
Sir M. HALE, 1664, with an Appendix by CHARLES CLARK, of Totham
Essex, 8vo. 1*s*
" The most perfect narrative of anything of this nature hitherto extant."—*Preface.*

Account of the Trial, Confession, and Condemnatio
of Six Witches at Maidstone, 1652 ; also the Trial and Execution of Thre
others at Faversham, 1645, 8vo. 1*s*
These Transactions are unnoticed by all Kentish historians.

An Essay on the Archæology of our Popula
Phrases and Nursery Rhymes, by H. B. KER, 2 vols. 12mo. *new cloth*, 4
(pub. at 12*s*)
A work which has met with great abuse among the reviewers, but those who are fond c
philological pursuits will read it now it is to be had at so very moderate a price, and it reall
contains a good deal of gossiping matter. The author's attempt is to explain every thin
from the Dutch, which he believes was the same language as the Anglo-Saxon.

The Merry Tales of the Wise Men of Gotham
edited by JAMES ORCHARD HALLIWELL, Esq. F.S.A., post 8vo. 1*s*

Miscellanies.

Illustrations of Eating, displaying the Omnivorou
Character of Man, and exhibiting the Natives of various Countries a
feeding-time, by a BEEF-EATER, fcap. 8vo. *with woodcuts*, 2*s*

Elements of Naval Architecture, being a Translatio
of the third part of CLAIRBOIS' " Traité Elémentairé de la Constructio
des Vaisseaux," by J. N. STRANGE, Commander, R.N., 8vo. *with* 5 *larg
folding plates, cloth*, 5*s*

Poems, partly of Rural Life (in National English)
by WILLIAM BARNES, Author of " Poems in the Dorset Dialect," 12mo
cloth, 5*s*

Waifs and Strays (a Collection of Poetry), 12mo
only 250 *printed, chiefly for presents, sewed*, 1*s* 6*d*

Book in the Press.

Facts and Speculations on the History of Playing
Cards in Europe, by W. A. CHATTO, Author of the ' History of Wood
Engraving, with Illustrations by J. Jackson,' 8vo. *profusely illustrated*

CPSIA information can be obtained
at www.ICGtesting.com
Printed in the USA
BVOW11s1003150817

492108BV00016B/188/P